PLAIN
TALK
ON

Deuteronomy

PLAIN TALK ON

Deuteronomy

MANFORD GEORGE GUTZKE
PH.D.

Lamplighter
Books Grand Rapids, Michigan
Zondervan Publishing House

Lamplighter Books are published by Zondervan Publishing House, 1415 Lake Drive, S.E., Grand Rapids, Michigan 49506

Library of Congress Cataloging in Publication Data

Gutzke, Manford George.
    Plain talk on Deuteronomy.

      1. Bible.   O.T.   Deuteronomy—Commentaries.
I.   Title.
BS1275.3.G87   222'.15'07   79-17813
ISBN 0-310-25691-7

Printed in the United States of America

84 85 86 87 88 — 10 9 8 7 6 5 4 3

CONTENTS

INTRODUCTION

✝   ✝   ✝

CONSECRATION IS THE WILL OF GOD

Do you think each Christian should be a consecrated person?

Salvation is the work of God in bringing a person out of the natural into the spiritual. Man cannot save himself; salvation is the developing of a relationship on the part of a human being with the person of God. We call saved persons Christians. The word *Christian* has about the same relation to the word *person* as *wife* has to *woman*. We understand that any wife is a woman, but we also know that not every woman is a wife. It takes a woman to be a wife, but no woman could be a wife by herself. So it is with the word *Christian:* one must be a human being to be a Christian, but not every human being is a Christian. Just as there is no wife without the woman having a husband, so there is no Christian without the person having Christ.

The gospel presents Christ as coming to man, calling man to Himself. A person does not just grow up and reach a point where he is in himself good enough to be called a Christian. A person must be born again. That is why the gospel is understood to be a call to man to come to God. Salvation is not a matter of God working in all people and eventually bringing them up to the Christian level. God confronts men by calling, "Come unto me," and promises to all who come, "I will give you rest." Christ's good news is that "whosoever will may come" and "whosoever cometh unto me, I will in no wise cast out."

We read in 2 Corinthians 5:17, "Therefore if any man be in Christ, he is a new creature." Thus we see that becoming a believer is actually a matter of being changed, of being inwardly regenerated by the grace and the power of God. Being

7

a believer, then, is not a special way of living that any human can conform to by his own efforts. Rather salvation involves a new relationship. For example, when a woman marries the routines of her life are not changed much: when single she had to keep house to a certain extent, but when she became married she began to clean and cook for two. Being married means she is no longer her own; she is now in fellowship with another. Similarly, when a person is born again he belongs to Christ and therefore serves Christ.

The revelation of the plan of salvation is seen in the history of Israel. The Israelites came out of Egypt, traveled across the desert, and entered the land of Canaan, the land of promise. They came *out of* the condition in which they were, *across* a temporary stage of learning, and *into* the land God had promised them. This is what happens in the course of being saved.

Salvation is the work of God the way a garden is the work of God, or the way a tree is the work of God. After the garden has been planted it must be fertilized, watered, and weeded. The result is vegetables and fruit from the garden.

In the spiritual life this is seen in such words as *conversion*, which takes place at the beginning; *growing*, which is the intermediate stage; and *consecration*, which is the final stage of yieldedness to God. Again, this is somewhat like getting married: after a time of courting, a couple has a joyous wedding, which is followed by years of growth and dedication to each other. Salvation is threefold: when a person accepts Christ he is saved from destruction, in Christ he is saved daily from yielding to the flesh; and by actually having the Lord with him, he is saved to living in Christ Jesus.

This concept can be seen clearly in Israel's history, as we shall study in the following chapters. The history of Israel, their salvation experience, began with being saved out of Egypt. From there they spent forty years wandering across the desert. Finally the Israelites were led across the river Jordan into the Promised Land. In our study of the Book of Deuteronomy we will be focusing on this final phase: entering into the land.

The children of Israel first came through the Red Sea where they were delivered from Pharaoh, who was destroyed when the sea closed over his army. Then they were brought across the desert guided with a cloud by day and fire by night. During this time they experienced the presence and help of God and lived under God's law that had been revealed on Mount Sinai. They were brought across the desert, learning and growing all the time. Finally they were led into the land. Here in spite of their earlier failures, they were helped by God to establish themselves in victorious control over the whole of Canaan.

Here we must notice a profound truth: the plan of God for Israel was not only to deliver them out of Egypt, but to bring them into the land of promise. But the sad and sobering fact is that many of them fell short of their goal. These things happened to them for our example, and they are written for our learning. Let us liken their example to apple blossoms. Each blossom has the potential of becoming an apple. As they grow some of the blossoms develop little green nubs that will eventually become apples. Finally, some grow mature fruit. The real danger in spiritual experience is that when a person feels free from doom, and knows that by the grace of God he will not go to hell, it is easy for him to fall into the snare of stopping short of bearing mature fruit and going on into the land of promise. Deuteronomy is a stirring call to believing people to press on to all that God wants them to have.

CHAPTERS 1–3

† † †

PAST HISTORY SHOWS FAILURE
(Deuteronomy 1)

Can we learn anything from the failures of the past?

Salvation is the work of God in bringing a person into living in Christ. When God saves men He not only saves them from hell, but He delivers them from the evil of this present world and brings them into eternal life, the life of the Lord Jesus Christ. There are people who become very interested and deeply stirred about becoming a believer, who yet have very little idea of what happens after a person believes. This suggests there are people who would be successful in coming out of Egypt but who would be unsuccessful entering into the land of Canaan.

The story of the Exodus is well known: many more came out of Egypt than entered Canaan. In the first of three addresses to the second generation of Israel in the Book of Deuteronomy, Moses recalls the Israelites' past. They had come out of Egypt, crossed through the sea and over the desert. They received the law at Mount Sinai and then moved on to Kadesh-Barnea, where Moses told them to go in and possess the land. Upon the report of their spies they decided they could not do it. At that point they turned back, and that whole disobedient generation died in the wilderness. Only Joshua and Caleb were spared to go into the land.

The experience of Israel prepares us for the sobering truth of what we might call arrested development. Unhappily not all who begin will finish. Paul emphasized this truth in his First Epistle to the Corinthians:

> Moreover, brethren, I would not that ye should be ignorant, how that all our fathers were under the cloud, and all passed

> through the sea; and were all baptized unto Moses in the cloud
> and in the sea; and did all eat the same spiritual meat; and did
> all drink the same spiritual drink . . . But with many of them
> God was not well pleased: for they were overthrown in the
> wilderness. Now these things were our examples, to the intent
> we should not lust after evil things, as they also lusted. . . .
> Now all these things happened unto them for ensamples: and
> they are written for our admonition, upon whom the ends of
> the world are come. Wherefore let him that thinketh he
> standeth take heed lest he fall (1 Cor. 10:1–12).

Here Paul warns against the possibility that a person can make
a good start yet have a poor finish. This does not mean that a
good start will mean a poor finish, but it does mean that after
you have made a good start you need to make good progress.

> For we are made partakers of Christ, if we hold the beginning
> of our confidence steadfast unto the end (Heb. 3:14).

Paul calls new believers babes in Christ, and often refers to
them as carnal. He points out that they should seek to become
mature in order that they may grow into the fullness of the
stature of their Savior, and be with Him in all life's experiences. This is the line of truth emphasized in Deuteronomy.

On the night that the Israelites left Egypt, the night of the
Passover, they probably had one thought in mind—to *reach*
Canaan and be free from slavery. But God had a different
point of view. He not only wanted His people to *reach* Canaan, but to *live* there. However, the truth we know from
history is that the first generation of people missed their potential heritage.

Deuteronomy is Moses' call to the second generation of
Israelites that they should achieve where the former generation had failed. Moses first reminded the people of their
former failure and the manner of it. He did this so that they
could make a healthy advance based on a realistic dependence
on God. In Deuteronomy 1:6–8 Moses points out to the
people that God had clearly called them to move forward.
God had given His promise that every place the soles of their
feet trod upon would be theirs. In verses 8–18 Moses tells
how the Israelites were organized and how he divided the
responsibility of leadership and allocated that responsibility so
that other persons had a part.

Verses 19–21 reveal that the moment of truth for the Israelites had passed; they had failed to trust God. Verses 22-25 show that the people wanted to send out spies to investigate the land and to plan the best means of entry. Moses agreed to this. Verses 26–40 record that Israel failed to go forward due to unbelief. This provoked God, and He shut them out of the land of Canaan, allowing only Caleb and Joshua to go in.

Moses reminded the people that they had tried to go forward in their own strength, bringing disaster and defeat upon themselves. God shut the door. This should be a warning to men. When God calls a person to Himself he is to come all the way over to God, to the place where he can have fellowship with God. Moses' review of failure was a warning against the peril that the Israelites might stop short of their goal. Modern day believers should learn from the failures of others so that they might do differently.

NEW GENERATION HAS NEW OPPORTUNITY
(Deuteronomy 2:1–23)

As you think of what you might undertake tomorrow, do you need to do anything about what happened yesterday?

Each new day brings its own importance in a person's life. We have the opportunity to decide today that tomorrow will be better than it was yesterday. Here in the second chapter of Deuteronomy we see that the Hebrews have an opportunity to go forward. But in this opportunity of going forward, of making up their minds today that they will do better tomorrow, they need to have in mind that what happened yesterday really counts. Some of what happens tomorrow will depend on the way we use today's opportunities, just as today's opportunities are somewhat affected by yesterday's actions. It is never wise to look forward into tomorrow without regard to what happened yesterday. We need to have this sober view of the guidance of God.

It is good for me to accept that I am today where God brought me. Maybe where I am is not where I might have been, but the fact that I am here now indicates that this is where God would have me to be. We must have this attitude about other people: they are as they are in the will and providence of God. People are as they are today because of what happened yesterday. As we move forward into a new day tomorrow we will have the wonderful opportunity to do better than we have ever done before. But we must recognize that the way in which we are now, is where we will start.

On one occasion David fled from the city of Jerusalem because his son, Absalom, had taken over the government and had led an insurrection in which David was driven out, threatened with death. The story goes that as David was passing through a certain valley in flight, one of his enemies by the name of Shimei stood on a hill and cursed him. One of David's generals offered to stop the man, but David said, "Let him curse. Maybe God told him to curse." Such an attitude is important, for a person will be faced by all kinds of troublesome characters and situations. When one has the frame of mind shown by David he can accept people as they are and give his personal attention to what God would have him do.

This concept is revealed in Deuteronomy 2:1–23 where God gives special guidance to the children of Israel. They encountered three different groups of people who were related to them in a sense: the children of Esau (the brother of Jacob), the children of Moab (who was one of the sons of Lot and a nephew of Abraham), and the children of Ammon (the other son of Lot). Moses gives Israel most amazing instructions:

> Ye are to pass through the coast of your brethren the children of Esau . . . Meddle not with them; for I will not give you of their land, no, not so much as a foot breadth; because I have given mount Seir unto Esau for a possession. Ye shall buy meat of them for money, that ye may eat; and ye shall also buy water of them for money, that ye may drink. For the Lord thy God hath blessed thee in all the works of thy hand: he knoweth thy walking through this great wilderness: these forty years the Lord thy God hath been with thee; thou hast lacked nothing (Deut. 2:4–7).

These natives were distant kinsmen who lived in the land before the Israelites came. Therefore Moses commanded the people to take nothing from them and in all their dealings recognize the natives for what they are. God would not give Israel any of the natives' land.

> And the Lord said unto me, Distress not the Moabites, neither contend with them in battle: for I will not give thee of their land for a possession; because I have given Ar unto the children of Lot for a possession (Deut. 2:9).

The same instructions were given to protect the children of Ammon. These three groups of people the children of Esau, the Moabites, and the Ammonites, were all kinsmen of Israel, and in that sense they were called brethren. They were the children of believers. Although they did not have glorious testimonies, they were not unbelievers. If we, like the children of Israel at this point, are to go forward into the fullness of the blessing of God we should recognize that there are other people in the world who also believe in God, even though they are different from us. In this day of many denominations this is a clear word: leave them alone. They have their church and their way of doing things. They say they believe in God, and that is not our business. We should accept the development of all the denominations as they are. I believe God is saying, "Do not dissipate your energies and distract your attention by seeking to coerce others into some uniformity of conduct. Just accept the fact that there will be other denominations. This does not mean that each of these groups sees the truth as well as others, but it means that the way they do and what they do is their business."

There will be people you must fight. Moses told the children of Israel which people they were to contend against—not other believers in God. The straight word of Moses at this point is "Mind your own business."

WAR AGAINST PAGAN ELEMENTS
(Deuteronomy 2:24–3:11)

Do you think a Christian should ever be dead set against anything?

If a believer wants to grow in his faith and really enter into the fullness of the gospel he must have a charitable attitude toward others.

This portion of Deuteronomy says that as the believer advances he must wage relentless war against carnal unbelief. He cannot afford to ever stop fighting against that which is contrary to the gospel of the Lord Jesus Christ. There may be in the community some ill-informed person full of zeal who preaches in a way other believers would not. He holds ideas about what it means to be a Christian that apparently are unwise, yet he believes in the Lord Jesus Christ. Other believers should look upon that person as a brother. They may not want to go to his services, but they can know that he is one with them. On the other hand, there may be even in the congregation a suave, cultured university professor, teaching perhaps in a men's Bible class, who does not accept the Bible as the Word of God. Believers must count that person as their enemy.

The portion of Scripture we are now considering will take us from 2:24 through 3:11.

> Rise ye up, take your journey, and pass over the river Arnon: behold, I have given unto thine hand Sihon the Amorite, king of Heshbon, and his land: begin to possess it, and contend with him in battle (Deut. 2:24).

Detailed instructions were given to seize the first opportunity to possess the land and to engage in battle for it.

> And the Lord said unto me, Behold, I have begun to give Sihon and his land before thee: begin to possess, that thou mayest inherit his land (Deut. 2:31).

Their prompt attack was successful.

> And we took all his cities at that time, and utterly destroyed the men, and the women, and the little ones, of every city, we left none to remain (Deut. 2:34).

The progress of their conquest in the land continued:

> So the Lord our God delivered into our hands Og also, the king of Bashan, and all his people: and we smote him until none was left to him remaining (Deut. 3:3).

In the history of the interpretation of the Bible there have been questions about the destruction of the Canaanites. Many scholars and Bible readers have wondered if this was really the plan of God. Sometimes it is said that it is the God of the Old Testament, as if it would be different in the New Testament; however, the New Testament speaks severely about anyone being led away spiritually. We must understand that "the cup of the Amorites"—their iniquity—was full, and God was prepared to get rid of these people because of their sins. Here is a practical illustration: Can you understand how it would be possible that a man should have his leg cut off so that he might live? When he was created he was given two legs but, circumstances have arisen under which one leg must be cut off at the knee in order that he might live. You may not believe in killing anything, but what about killing disease germs that a man may live?

In the world there is that which is good and that which is bad. There is that which is vital and helpful to life, and there is that which is fatal. Destructive elements do exist and they call for stern countermeasures. God is the Judge and we must be ready to walk with Him in judgment. In Titus 1:10-11 we find that Paul told Titus there were teachers "whose mouths must be stopped, who subvert whole houses." There was to be no fellowship with unbelief.

RESPONSIBILITY AND LEADERSHIP
(Deuteronomy 3:12–29)

Do some persons have a special responsibility to help others come nearer to God?

Salvation is the work of God in bringing us to Himself by His Word. There may be many who, as they look forward into tomorrow, are wondering if they have to live their lives the way other people have done in the past. Many people say they are Christians, yet they live weak and fruitless lives. They seldom pray or read the Bible or really walk with the Lord. Would you like to come closer to God and be among those who really walk with Him? Coming into the presence of God and having fellowship with Him is the real objective of salvation.

Anybody, any place, is dealt with so far as God is concerned on the basis of what he does. "Whatsoever a man soweth, that shall he also reap" (Gal. 6:7). We know that sin has ruined the natural heart of man. In the flesh man is lost because "all have sinned and come short of the glory of God" (Rom. 3:23). But we rejoice in the wonderful truth of the Gospel: the Son of man has come "to seek and to save that which was lost" (Luke 19:10). By the grace of God we are saved through faith and that not of ourselves: it is the gift of God (Eph. 2:8). And we rejoice to tell the world that "whosoever believeth in Him shall not perish but have everlasting life" (John 3:16).

Believing in God includes a learning process. We start by finding out about God—accepting the things of God, yielding to the truth of God, and then obeying the will of God. Salvation may be illustrated as follows: A man falls into a river and is about to drown. While he flounders in the water a lifeboat comes along beside him. He is helped into the lifeboat which will take him to safety. No man can be a believer by himself. He must hear from someone who knows the gospel what the Lord Jesus Christ will do for him. Coming to faith is a gradual thing, like the growing of a plant or the developing of a person. Beginning by putting faith in Christ, a person then grows as a sapling, and finally he is mature as a tree and bears fruit. A human being starts out as a babe, grows as a child, becomes a young lad and finally comes into maturity. The same thing happens spiritually.

> For we are made partakers of Christ, if we hold the beginning
> of our confidence steadfast unto the end (Heb. 3:14).

After one has accepted Christ and is a babe in Christ, he is to desire the sincere milk of the Word that he may grow thereby. Just as one is brought to Christ by those who know Him, so a person is brought nearer to Christ by those who are near to Him.

It is well to keep in mind that people are different. Some people are given special talents or positions for helping others draw close to Christ. These ones will be rewarded according to how they fulfill their responsibility. Those who come from a Bible-believing home or are brought up in a Bible-believing church fellowship are responsible to help those who do not know the Bible that they, too, might come close to God. This truth is set forth in the portion of Deuteronomy to which our attention is drawn now.

In 3:12–29 we find that Moses has something to say to certain people who had special privileges. As the Israelites came from the desert they arrived at the country where Sihon, the king of the Amorites, and Og, the king of Bashan, ruled. In the fighting that took place Israel was victorious. They were now ready to cross over the river Jordan into the land of Canaan, where they would have to fight every step of the way to gain possession. While they were poised on the riverbank two tribes, Reuben and Gad, came to Moses and asked for the privilege of settling in the country where Sihon and Og had been conquered. If they settled there it would give them a big advantage because there they would be safe. Moses allowed them to settle there, but he made a condition: those who were able to fight were to go fully armed in the front rank of the other tribes when they crossed the river Jordan. They were to fight their enemies until each of the ten tribes were settled; then they could return home.

Reuben and Gad were required to fight not only their own battles but also the battles of others. This is what people with special privileges should do. Reuben and Gad were told that "until the Lord hath given rest unto your brethren, as well as unto you" they were to be in the forefront of battle.

We see another example of this responsibility in that since Moses was not allowed to go into the land, and Joshua was the one person especially fitted to lead, Moses was to charge and encourage him and to strengthen him.

When a believer is going forward into the fullness of spiritual blessing, part of his responsibility will be to help those not as fortunate as he is. Those who want to get ahead will get ahead by being responsibile for the progress of those who are less fortunate.

CHAPTER 4

† † †

CAREFUL OBEDIENCE TO THE REVEALED WORD
(Deuteronomy 4:1–9)

Is it important for a Christian to live strictly by every commandment and example in the Bible?

The Bible was given to believers to guide them in obedience to God. Far different from what the world might think, the Bible was never meant to be an argument to convince unbelievers. We need to be careful about this; it is easy for us to be snared by the world. Sometimes knowingly and sometimes unknowingly, unbelievers generate questions that challenge us for an answer. When we fall into their trap and try to give answers to questions they raise, we often do not realize they could not understand the answer even if we told them the truth.

We can learn this from the Lord Himself. When did He ever argue with an unwilling man? At no time did He have anything to do with a man who did not want to believe. It is easy to think that good answers will win converts, but that is not true. Many people are not unbelievers for lack of information but for lack of interest.

The one short, simple word the Bible speaks to the whole world is *repent*; and if they want a second word it is *believe*. That is all we are authorized to say to the world outside. Some Christians start conversations with unbelievers by asking, what do you think God is like? what do you think God will do? what do you think heaven is like, or hell? None of this really makes much difference. The question that matters is this: what is your relationship with God? With reference to the Lord Jesus Christ, what attitude do you have toward Him?

Once a person has accepted Jesus as Lord he begins to walk in the way of the Lord, a process that needs to be learned. The believer, seeking to know and obey the will of his Lord, will need instruction. Some people may put it this way: the dynamic of Christian living is the love of Christ. The direction of Christian living is in His Word. Scripture says:

> Eye hath not seen, nor ear heard, neither have entered into the heart of man, the things which God hath prepared for them that love him. But God hath revealed them unto us by his Spirit (1 Cor. 2:9-10).

The language Moses uses here in Deuteronomy warns of human tendencies to direct one's own life.

> Now therefore hearken, O Israel, unto the statutes and unto the judgments, which I teach you, for to do them, that ye may live, and go in and possess the land (Deut. 4:1).

In order to go in and possess the lands the Israelites needed to listen and obey. Disobedience could bring death. Men today must activate the revealed Word of God in their own lives.

There must be many Bible students, and perhaps even preachers, who never read this passage:

> Ye shall not add unto the word which I command you, neither shall ye diminish ought from it, that ye may keep the commandments of the Lord your God which I command you (Deut. 4:2).

Isn't that plain? Do not add to it, and do not take away from it. When I read that I am not thinking of single words, or of adding one single phrase or syllable. I do not think that is what is meant here. The idea is to not bring any new ideas to be added to those which have been revealed. People have various procedures for diminishing the Bible. Some study the New Testament and decline to study the Old Testament. Others will omit references to passages they don't understand or agree with. Some believe they can be in good fellowship with God and actually be one of His own people yet pay no attention at all to the quality of life they live. We are to enter into the fullness of the blessing of God in a way that people in the past did not, by taking the revealed Word of God and go exactly by that.

> Keep therefore and do them; for this is your wisdom and your
> understanding in the sight of the nations (Deut. 4:6).

Abide by the Word of God and people will see that you are
wise. This is your valid claim to recognition among other
people.

> Only take heed to thyself, and keep thy soul diligently, lest
> thou forget the things which thine eyes have seen, and lest
> they depart from thy heart all the days of thy life: but teach
> them thy sons, and thy sons' sons (Deut. 4:9).

Here we could underscore word for word. "Take heed to
thyself"—watch out; "keep thy soul diligently"—be careful
what you think—"lest thou forget the things which thine eyes
have seen." You have learned scriptural truths. Remember
them, and teach them to your children and your grandchil-
dren. Careful control of the heart to remember and to obey
will be established as you teach your own children.

DISREGARD NATURAL ELEMENTS
IN REVELATION
(Deuteronomy 4:10–24)

Should we separate the human elements from the divine in
the Bible?

The spiritual desire of every believer is to be closer to the
Lord. All who believe agree that the common prayer of the
heart is, "Lord, increase our faith." Faith is not magical; there
is nothing mysterious in the way it comes. Faith can get
stronger and it can get weaker, but faith is not willpower.
Faith is a genuine response in obedience to God's revealed
will, but it can be nurtured. You can learn more about what
the Lord's will is for you, and you can be more inclined to
believe that if you trust Him He will accomplish it. Moses was
doing this in the Book of Deuteronomy. He was trying to get
the Israelites to draw nearer to God, so they could move into
the land of promise where their parents had failed to do so.

Believing in God is directly related to receiving the Bible as the Word of God. All faith is not faith in God. When the Bible speaks about believing, it means believing in God according to His promises. If you do not know the promises of God you will not believe in them. Paul says in Romans:

> For whosoever shall call upon the name of the Lord shall be saved. How then shall they call on him in whom they have not believed? and how shall they believe in him of whom they have not heard? (Rom. 10:13–14).

Do you see the point? You cannot believe in God or in the Lord Jesus Christ unless you have heard about them. How will you hear? Why not take the Bible, the Word of God, and learn? The Bible came through holy men who were moved by the Holy Ghost (2 Peter 1:20-21).

Israel had received God's Word through Moses, but they did not respond in obedience. Therefore Israel did not qualify for the blessing and so enter in and possess the land of Canaan. This is very serious. It means that a person can actually begin believing in God and yet stop short of the full blessing intended. Believing is the attitude of heart with which the believer takes to himself what is promised through Christ Jesus. After you learn what the Bible says about the Lord Jesus Christ, receive and stand on it: that is believing.

Those who came out of Egypt and traveled through the wilderness lived in unbelief. Moses gave certain warnings from God to guide this new generation. In the last part of chapter 4 Moses shows that the former generation had misinterpreted some things about the Word of God as revealed to them.

> Take ye therefore good heed unto yourselves; for ye saw no manner of similitude on the day that the Lord spake unto you in Horeb out of the midst of the fire: lest ye corrupt yourselves, and make you a graven image (Deut. 4:15-16).

They were to take heed to themselves about what? Apparently they were to be careful about what they thought.

The English word *similitude* is not a very common one. It means "likeness." They did not see anything they could recognize on the day that the Lord spake to them. What Moses is saying to them is that on the day the Lord spoke on Mount Sinai they did not see anything particularly human about it; they did not see any bodily form. Yet in their own minds the people conjured up an image of what the voice they heard belonged to. And that is where the warning comes: take heed to yourself and be careful that when you think on the Word of God you do not develop wrong ideas in your mind about the human elements God used to reveal His Word. For instance, someone might say, "It was just Moses who gave us that." You may ask me, "Well, wasn't it Moses?" Yes, Moses did instruct the people in the commandments, but his words were not his own; they were God's. I can illustrate it like this: suppose a telegram from a friend is brought to your house by a small boy. Does that change the message? Or, if an elderly man brought it to you, does that change the telegram? You see, the person who brings it does not change the message. In handling the Scripture, if anyone looks for the human elements he will be spiritually corrupted. That is the warning we have here.

The important thing is that God saved His people.

> But the Lord hath taken you, and brought you forth out of the iron furnace, even out of Egypt, to be unto him a people of inheritance, as ye are this day (Deut. 4:20).

We are not to dwell on the human elements involved; we are to consider what God actually did. We must remember that God is the author of the Bible; men are merely His writing instruments. It may help us to know something of the background of the Bible writers, but we must never say this is Moses' word or Paul's word, for the Bible is entirely the Word of God.

CONSTANT PRIVILEGE OF REPENTANCE
(Deuteronomy 4:25–49)

Do you know the one thing you can do every time you do wrong?

The truth we find pictured in Deuteronomy of the life of Israel is written for us that we may learn from their experiences. The Israelites were called of God and were known as

God's people. God brought them out of Egypt across the wilderness into Canaan where they were to be free and where they were to be blessed. But two years after they were brought out of Egypt, at Kadesh-Barnea they failed to go into the land because of unbelief. This reveals that one may start out in faith, believing in God and in the Lord Jesus Christ, understanding that Christ Jesus died for him and that Jesus' blood will take away sins. But when he finds that he now belongs to Christ and must walk with Him, trusting Him in every way, he fails. People with this experience must learn that the same power that will bring them out of the natural, is the same power that will bring them into the spiritual. The power of God that delivers us from sins is the same power of God that brings us into His will by His Holy Spirit.

In this portion of Deuteronomy we are reminded that the former generation failed to enter Canaan because they did not believe. It was now necessary for the new generation to avoid mistakes of the older generation. Moses has reviewed the failures of the past and has held them up as a warning. The Israelite spies returned and told the people about giants in the land, and they felt weak; they were like grasshoppers, and before those high-walled cities they had no strength. Do you recognize how human this is? The same is true for unbelievers today. For example, in a home where there is family trouble and the members try to solve their conflicts without God's principles and help, they will never have any real assurance that they will live in peace. They will go from one sad day to the next, feeling defeated, and because they have no faith in the Lord, He will not be able to help them.

Now let us come back to the story here. After he had reminded them of their failures of the past, Moses gave careful admonition to the Israelites. In previous chapters we have noticed such things as this: they were told not to meddle with Esau, Moab, or Ammon, relatives of the Hebrews (we can think of them as other believers). They were told not to try to force those people into their way of doing things. At the same time they were told not to spare Sihon, the king of the Amorites, or Og, the king of Bashan. They were to be absolutely opposed to these pagans.

The Israelites were also told that they should expect certain persons to lead. Reuben and Gad were favored over the others because they were given their possessions on the desert side of the river Jordan. But they were given responsibility to lead in the battles for the others, and to work for their brothers. Joshua was now being charged, and given grace and strength that he should take up where Moses left off and go into the land. The people were then given specific instructions to move along by the revealed Word of God. But in the event of their doing wrong, the Israelites could get right with God through repentance.

> When thou shalt beget children, and children's children, and ye shall have remained long in the land, and shall corrupt yourselves, and make a graven image, or the likeness of any thing, and shall do evil in the sight of the Lord thy God, to provoke him to anger: I call heaven and earth to witness against you this day, that ye shall soon utterly perish from off the land whereunto ye go over Jordan to possess it; ye shall not prolong your days upon it, but shall utterly be destroyed. And the Lord shall scatter you among the nations, and ye shall be left few in number among the heathen, whither the Lord shall lead you. And there ye shall serve gods, the work of men's hands, wood and stone, which neither see, nor hear, nor eat, nor smell. But if from thence thou shalt seek the Lord thy God, thou shalt find him, if thou seek him with all thy heart and with all thy soul (Deut. 4:25-29).

We should look at verse 29 again and again! And then we read:

> When thou art in tribulation, and all these things are come upon thee, even in the latter days, if thou turn to the Lord thy God, and shalt be obedient unto his voice; (for the Lord thy God is a merciful God;) he will not forsake thee, neither destroy thee, nor forget the covenant of thy fathers which he sware unto them (Deut. 4:30-31).

This is another wonderful promise of God. In the latter part of this chapter we read that the Israelites were to set aside three cities of mercy for people who committed crimes. If when we sin we will repent, God will always forgive us.

CHAPTERS 5–7

† † †

REPEATED TEN WORDS ARE
EXACTLY THE SAME
(Deuteronomy 5:1–22)

If a person repeats himself, saying something in exactly the same words he used the first time, what does that indicate?

The revealed Word of God, the Bible, means exactly what it says. When you say something and someone does not hear well, he will ask you to repeat it. And you may or may not use the same words over. If you do use the same words you probably meant exactly what you said.

Deuteronomy is made up of two words: *Deuter* means "second" and *onomy* means "law." This book then refers to the second giving of the law. The first giving of the law, of course, was at Mount Sinai, when Moses went up on the mount and brought down the tablets of stone. The first tablets were smashed, but he went back for the second tablets which were just like the first ones. The Book of Deuteronomy tells of the second giving of the law, thirty-eight years later, to the new generation just before they entered into the Promised Land.

This is very significant to us. Every generation needs to hear the gospel all over again. We notice here that when Moses did give the law the second time, it was exactly the same as the first time, word for word. This was a new generation, many of whom were born in the wilderness and probably never were slaves—but the Word was the same.

> These words the Lord spake unto all your assembly in the mount out of the midst of the fire, of the cloud, and of the thick darkness, with a great voice: and he added no more. And he wrote them in two tables of stone, and delivered them unto me (Deut. 5:22).

I go over that phrase again and again until it rings in my soul. "He added no more." Why? He had said it; the Word of God was "settled forever in heaven."

Many, in a world where there is so much change, ask how can God's Word stay the same? Many maintain that God's Word is bound to be modified to some extent. How could it be the same? I will tell you: we have the same God, and He never changes. Grounded into His very being and because He is as He is, His Word will remain as it is. This is why, in studying the Bible, we need to find out what the Bible actually says, because what the Bible says is God speaking. Down through the generations He has said, "Come unto me" and He says it now, and it means the same. Events change, but the principles of life and the things that are eternal do not change. The Ten Commandments given on Mount Sinai that were afterwards repeated on the occasion of the children of Israel entering Canaan reveal the eternal nature of God.

Some years ago, while attending a conference, someone asked me if I did not think that in the passing of hundreds and hundreds of years God would have other things to reveal, and I made the comment, "If He would send the Lord Jesus Christ back here to live a little longer, leaving the Lord Jesus Christ to do it differently on Calvary, then we will say there is some change in the revelation. But when the Lord Jesus Christ on Calvary as He was dying said, 'It is finished,' I believe Him. Period! That is the end of it so far as God is concerned, and I do not think there was ever added one other thing." The events in the life of Jesus Christ are the whole truth about God and His attitude toward us.

AUTHORIZED TEACHING IS VALID
(Deuteronomy 5:23–33)

How can any ordinary person learn about God?

The revealed Word of God can be shared person to person. In the Book of Deuteronomy we have been concerned with

Israel successfully entering into Canaan. The former generation had failed, but God's promises were sure and His will would now be done. When Moses talked about the former generation he was not trying to give them a bad name, nor was he taking pleasure in their mistakes. He wanted the new generation to avoid the pitfalls of their ancestors.

In this exposition I will occasionally refer to former generations of Christians, but I have no hesitation in saying that I do not think the Christian church of my generation has entered into the fullness of the blessing as it could. I do not want to make the former church look bad but want to encourage you to enter in where other people—the former generation—failed to go. It can be done, but as Moses points out, the only way you will ever make it where the others failed, is when you avoid the pitfalls.

We evangelicals have the Bible in our hands, and we belong to those people who think that everybody has the privilege to come to God in the Lord Jesus Christ and be saved. We are "the priesthood of all believers." This means that each man who is a believer can have personal access into the presence of God. This is not just a privilege we can assume if we want to; it is the responsibility we are to assume because it is assigned to us. We should come into the presence of God and intercede on behalf of other people. The Lord Jesus Christ came into this world to seek and to save the lost, and He gave Himself as a ransom for many. He said to His disciples, "As my Father hath sent me, even so send I you" (John 20:21). We are to come into the presence of God as priests and pray for other people, seeking to reconcile them to God. But what has happened? Earlier generations never did enter into the promises that were before them. This generation could do it. If people would study the Bible and have fellowship with the Lord there would be effectual witnessing.

Moses, in Deuteronomy 5, reminds the people that they requested that he should be their minister—the one who was to go before God.

> Go thou near, and hear all that the Lord our God shall say: and speak thou unto us all that the Lord our God shall speak unto thee; and we will hear it, and do it. And the Lord heard the voice of your words, when ye spake unto me; and the Lord said unto me, I have heard the voice of the words of this people,

> which they have spoken unto thee: they have well said all that
> they have spoken (Deut. 5:27-28).

God approved this arrangement and said that it was a good
thing. In a pathetic outcry God says that He really wants to
bless.

> O that there were such a heart in them, that they would fear
> me, and keep all my commandments always, that it might be
> well with them, and with their children for ever! (Deut. 5:29).

Then the Lord God told Moses to guide the people into their
tents again. They could depend on the outcome.

> But as for thee, stand thou here by me, and I will speak unto
> thee all the commandments, and the statutes, and the judg-
> ments, which thou shalt teach them, that they may do them in
> the land which I give them to possess it. Ye shall observe to do
> therefore as the Lord your God hath commanded you: ye shall
> not turn aside to the right hand or to the left. Ye shall walk in
> all the ways which the Lord your God hath commanded you,
> that ye may live, and that it may be well with you, and that ye
> may prolong your days in the land which ye shall possess
> (Deut. 5:31–33).

That is a promise for everyone. We do not have Moses, but
we do have the Bible, the authorized messenger. A believer
can stand on the Bible and on what it says: "Walk in all its
ways and all will be well with you." What does the Bible say?
When the Lord Jesus Christ was asked by His disciples,
"What shall we do, that we might work the works of God?"
His answer was, "This is the work of God, that ye believe on
him whom he hath sent" (John 6:28, 29). That is the whole
message of the Bible. Put your trust in the Lord and He will
take care of you.

THOU AND THY HOUSE KEEP THE WORD
(Deuteronomy 6:1–9)

Is there such a thing as a Christian talking about the Bible too
much in his home with his own family?

What we are seeing here in Deuteronomy is God's aim to

lead the Israelites into fuller blessing. You and I can benefit from these passages. Perhaps things you expected to do when you first became a Christian, you have not done; the way you thought you were going to live you have not carried out. You probably thought you would read your Bible regularly and earnestly exercise yourself in prayer. You probably thought you would invite other people to church, and that in general you would act like a Christian. But that did not happen. In your case you do not have to expect that you will die in the desert while another generation goes forward; you can change your way right now. It is good for us to keep in mind that salvation, this great work of God in bringing us to Himself, is received by faith. And faith comes by hearing and hearing by the Word of God.

In the first nine verses of chapter 6 Moses puts his finger on this crucial point. He has in mind that these people will go into the land to achieve something their forefathers never achieved, and they will need faith. Learning the Word of God, that is, learning the Scriptures, is very much like learning a new language. Have you ever thought about how a baby learns to speak? The baby hears words over and over. The Bible has an expression for it, "Line upon line, precept upon precept, here a little, there a little."

The following passage tells us a number of things that we are to do: we are to teach the Word of God, and we are to follow it. In the course of doing it we will fear the Lord, keep all His commandments, show honor and reverence, and be obedient.

> Now these are the commandments, the statutes, and the judgments, which the Lord your God commanded to teach you, that ye might do them in the land whither ye go to possess it: that thou mightest fear the Lord thy God, to keep all his statutes and his commandments, which I command thee, thou, and thy son, and thy son's son, all the days of thy life; and that thy days may be prolonged (Deut. 6:1-2).

Notice the order here: first, we are taught the commandments, and then we practice them. In that way we learn to reverence God, and as we reverence Him we become obedient. We will try in every possible way to do all that is pleasing in the sight of the Lord.

> Hear therefore, O Israel, and observe to do it; that it may be
> well with thee, and that ye may increase mightily. . . (Deut.
> 6:3).

If God's people do the will of God and obey His Word, He
will bless them, and they will increase mightily.

> And thou shalt love the Lord thy God with all thine heart, and
> with all thy soul, and with all thy might. And these words,
> which I command thee this day, shall be in thine heart: and
> thou shalt teach them diligently unto thy children, and shalt
> talk of them when thou sittest in thine house, and when thou
> walkest by the way, and when thou liest down, and when thou
> risest up (Deut. 6:5–7).

This passage points out that loving God is not a matter of
sentiment but of obeying His laws. And herein is love, that
you keep His commandments. In your heart you will want to
obey Him, and thus you will keep His commandments. You
will have these words deep down inside yourself that they
may guide you.

"And thou shalt teach them diligently unto thy children."
One way to get the commandments of God deep down into
your heart is to talk about them to your loved ones.

> And thou shalt bind them for a sign upon thine hand, and they
> shall be as frontlets between thine eyes (Deut. 6:8).

Binding them for a sign upon the hand is like making a
bracelet of them and putting it on the wrist, and a frontlet is
like having a medal hanging on the forehead with the Word of
God printed on it.

> And thou shalt write them upon the posts of thy house, and on
> thy gates (Deut. 6:9).

This passage suggests putting up signs everywhere. God's
commandments will be deep within our hearts if we are surrounded by them.

At the beginning of this meditation I asked whether you
think there is such a thing as a Christian talking about the
Bible too much. I imagine a person can talk about it in a
tiresome way; but to continue bringing the truths of Scripture up before others is good—good for you and good for
others.

DO NOT FORGET GOD IN YOUR PROSPERITY
(Deuteronomy 6:10–25)

Do you realize how easy it is to forget the help that was given to you?

Walking in the will of God will result in much blessing. The nearer we are to Him the more we will be blessed. Any human being in himself is surrounded by difficulties that are too much for him. He is too foolish in his own understanding and too weak in his own strength to do the things he should do. Therefore he turns to God, trusts in His grace and mercy, and finds help from God. The result is victory in God, bringing peace and joy to the once troubled believer. Danger lies in that the believer will forget the help given him and take the glory for himself. In actuality the believer has nothing that he did not receive from God.

Moses had this thought in mind when he was dealing with the Israelites. He was leading them into something better than anything their forefathers had. They would be led into achievement in spiritual matters. Moses warned the people that as they moved forward to enter into the fullness of the blessing of God, they must not forget God, who helped them as they achieved one victory after another.

> And it shall be, when the Lord thy God shall have brought thee into the land . . . to give thee great and goodly cities, which thou buildest not, and houses full of all good things, which thou filledst not, and wells digged, which thou diggedst not, vineyards and olive trees, which thou plantedst not; when thou shalt have eaten and be full; then beware lest thou forget the Lord, which brought thee forth out of the land of Egypt, from the house of bondage (Deut. 6:10–12).

They were receiving houses and cities they had not built, wells they had not dug, vineyards and olive trees they had not planted; but Moses emphasizes they are to remember the God who gave them those blessings, the God who brought them out of the land of Egypt.

When we thank and praise God, it should be not so much for the fact that He helped yesterday, and that He is taking care of us and has blessed us in many ways; but for saving our souls, for giving His Son to die for us, because with that came everything else.

> Thou shalt fear the Lord thy God, and serve him, and shalt
> swear by his name (Deut. 6:13).

The believer is to make the Lord his God and put his trust in
Him. The word *fear* does not mean that he will be afraid in
any slavish way—he will think of the way God helps and be
greatly stirred, not giving the credit to other gods.

> Ye shall not go after other gods, of the gods of the people which
> are round about you; (for the Lord thy God is a jealous God
> among you) lest the anger of the Lord thy God be kindled
> against thee, and destroy thee from off the face of the earth
> (Deut. 6:14–15).

This is a sober warning, and what is the danger here? That
when a believer has received blessing he will give the credit
to something the unbelieving public also would. A believer
could forfeit his privilege of blessing by ascribing credit to
natural processes when it was God's help that really made the
difference in his life.

> Ye shall not tempt the Lord your God. . . . Ye shall diligently
> keep the commandments of the Lord your God, and his tes-
> timonies, and his statutes, which he hath commanded thee.
> And thou shalt do that which is right and good in the sight of
> the Lord: that it may be well with thee, and that thou mayest
> go in and possess the good land which the Lord sware unto thy
> fathers, to cast out all thine enemies from before thee, as the
> Lord hath spoken (Deut. 6:16–19).

Have you been blessed in your home, and do you have a sense
of quietness when you pray? Are you able to turn matters over
to God? Well, give God thanks. And remember, if you trust in
the Lord and are patient, you are not patient because your
grandfather was a good man; you are patient because God is
giving you His grace to strengthen you. The inward dynamic,
the urge to do the will of God, comes from the Lord God
Himself. You should be careful to show this to your children.

> And when thy son asketh thee in time to come, saying, What
> mean the testimonies, and the statutes, and the judgments,
> which the Lord our God hath commanded you? Then thou
> shalt say unto thy son, We were Pharaoh's bondmen in Egypt;
> and the Lord brought us out of Egypt with a mighty hand
> (Deut. 6:20-21).

It is important never to forget God and His original way of

dealing with you and saving your soul. We must always remember that every good thing comes to us from the Lord God, who gave His Son to die for us. One good way not to forget God and His help, is to tell your children how He redeemed you at Calvary's cross. Give Him the glory.

SALVATION AND PROSPERITY COME BY GRACE
(Deuteronomy 7:1–5)

Do you know that becoming a believer is not the result of any natural process?

When a man becomes a believer certain good things follow in his life, especially as he draws nearer to the Lord. Life, the way you and I live it, is pretty much a battle. There are things that are for us, and things that are against us, and the way we live from day to day is not always easy. Moses was anxious that the children of Israel should remember the part God had taken in their affairs. He pointed out that they were to be always conscious of the fact that it was God who was blessing them. The tendency to look for natural or personal causes for success can lead the heart away from God. In order to grow in grace and knowledge the believer needs to recognize that it is the Lord who helps him.

When God gave the victory over natural factors to Israel He instructed them to utterly repudiate any appreciation of those elements:

> When the Lord thy God shall bring thee into the land whither thou goest to possess it, and hath cast out many nations before thee . . . seven nations greater and mightier than thou; and when the Lord thy God shall deliver them before thee; thou shalt smite them, and utterly destroy them; thou shalt make no covenant with them, nor shew mercy unto them: neither shalt thou make marriages with them; thy daughter thou shalt not give unto his son, nor his daughter shalt thou take unto thy son. For they will turn away thy son from following me, that they may serve other gods: so will the anger of the Lord be kindled against you, and destroy thee suddenly (Deut. 7:1–4).

There are factors in situations with which you and I have to deal that are no help to us in spiritual matters. Believers become the Lord's own, and walk with Him in spite of those things. Believers should not allow themselves to give credit to anyone or anything but God. Paul manifested this personal attitude.

> Though I might also have confidence in the flesh. If any other man thinketh that he hath whereof he might trust in the flesh, I more: circumcised the eighth day, of the stock of Israel, of the tribe of Benjamin, a Hebrew of the Hebrews; as touching the law, a Pharisee; concerning zeal, persecuting the church; touching the righteousness which is in the law, blameless (Phil. 3:4–6).

Each of those attributes in Paul's time would have been considered good, but his attitude was: "But what things were gain to me, those I counted loss for Christ" (Phil. 3:7).

Some persons, when they draw near to the Lord, and when they grow in spiritual matters, are tempted to think this is because of their family upbringing. Their parents, grandparents, brothers, and sisters were good Christians, so naturally they are good Christians because they are in this family. But that is not true. If one is actually close to God, it will be because of the Lord Jesus Christ, who died for him. Perhaps some may think the reason they have good fortune is because of their generosity with money, inasmuch as they are able to give to missions and other worthy causes. But it is not the money that makes a soul right before God; it is the Lord Jesus Christ who makes the believer right before God. The justified believer can use the money for God's glory.

Moses gives a sober warning:

> For they will turn away thy son from following me, that they may serve other gods (Deut. 7:4).

Esteem for natural elements will affect children. It is tragic to see believers who are personally trusting in the Lord fill their homes with all kinds of worldly treasures, all the evidences of what money can buy and culture can bring. Often children become worldly because they are surrounded with material things. Believing parents must use godly discretion when spending their money.

YOU BELONG ONLY TO GOD
(Deuteronomy 7:6–26)

What attitude should a believer have toward the world?

Salvation makes a man belong in another world. Just as there is earth, so there is heaven; just as there is the natural, so there is the spiritual; and just as there is the temporal, so there is the eternal. Being a believer is more than being a man. Every Christian is a human being, but not every human being is a Christian. The human being who has Jesus Christ is the Christian, and his citizenship is in heaven.

As Moses was preparing Israel for entrance into the fullness of salvation (and that is what going into the Promised Land means) he emphasized the importance of their recognizing that when they were in Canaan they would be separated unto God from other people in Canaan. There should always be a difference between God's people and the people of the world. The children of Israel would have dealings with the Canaanites, but they were to achieve and to maintain control over them; they were not to allow the Canaanites to influence them.

In Deuteronomy 7 we find Moses saying that the blessing of God would make His people prosper, so that they would be "blessed above all people."

> And the Lord will take away from thee all sickness, and will put none of the evil diseases of Egypt, which thou knowest, upon thee; but will lay them upon all them that hate thee. And thou shalt consume all the people which the Lord thy God shall deliver thee; thine eye shall have no pity upon them: neither shalt thou serve their gods; for that will be a snare unto thee (Deut. 7:15–16).

Often, when people read this, they feel this sounds very harsh. But it is a matter of life and death. The amputation of a man's leg, if he has gangrene in the foot or the leg, is harsh, but that is the only way to save his life. It is not easy; and by the way, the servant is not greater than his Master. It was not easy for the sinless Jesus of Nazareth to bear on the cross of Calvary the sins of mankind.

Moses told these people as they prepared to go into the land of Canaan that they would be spared evil diseases, which would mark them as fortunate, but they must not allow their human sympathy to snare them into participation with the worldly Canaanites. We will be different from other people. When you consider the impressive strength of all that which is worldly, and when you consider the great number of people who do not attend church, and you see the great wealth and power of those who do things in their own way, you should not be dismayed. Rather you should remember you are not confident about your future because you are strong; you are confident because God is all powerful and will help you.

> But the Lord thy God shall deliver them unto thee, and shall destroy them with a mighty destruction, until they be destroyed (Deut. 7:23).

Victory over natural elements is a gradual thing; it does not all come at once. The believer will never have his way in this world or be able to change others' way of living, but he will be delivered from the burden and will enter into the joy of his Lord, having the peace of God that passeth understanding. The believer can have daily blessing from God and in himself will win the victory.

In verses 23 and 24 the ultimate victory over all natural factors is assured. God will give the complete victory to His people. Then in verses 25 and 26 Moses reveals that God's people were not to make any personal profit out of this victory. Thus we learn that we should put our trust in the Lord, and if we want to know the fullness of His blessing, we should make a difference between ourselves and other people.

Any community has social events. and many of these have sinfulness in them. As a believer we will be better off not taking part in these activities. We should walk with the Lord and not let our personal interests move us to have dealings with the people of this world.

CHAPTERS 8 and 9

✝ ✝ ✝

REMEMBER YOUR PAST
(Deuteronomy 8:1–9)

How important is it to remember the past?

In moving forward to be closer to the Lord it is helpful to keep past experiences in mind. When we look back into our lives it is not difficult to see the hand of God in many things and to feel confident of God's blessing, yet when we look ahead we become uncertain. In addition to looking ahead we need to look up to God. As we draw nearer to God what can we expect? How will God deal with us? We get our answer by looking at what He has done in the past, how He has brought us to this point. The way He dealt with us yesterday is the way He will deal with us tomorrow. When we think on this we will have courage to go forward.

> All the commandments which I command thee this day shall ye observe to do, that ye may live, and multiply, and go in and possess the land which the Lord sware unto your fathers. And thou shalt remember all the way which the Lord thy God led thee these forty years in the wilderness, to humble thee, and to prove thee, to know what was in thine heart, whether thou wouldest keep his commandments, or no. And he humbled thee, and suffered thee to hunger, and fed thee with manna, which thou knewest not, neither did thy fathers know; that he might make thee know that man doth not live by bread only, but by every word that proceedeth out of the mouth of the Lord doth man live (Deut. 8:1–3).

This Scripture passage is the one Jesus quoted when He was being tempted by Satan to make stones into bread.

Moses points out that God led the Hebrews in the wilderness and dealt with them in such a way as to impress this great truth on them. While we are here in this world we are also in the spiritual world, and the Lord God leads us through experiences on earth to impress on our minds that while it is true that the body lives by bread, it is also true that the soul of man lives by every word that proceeds out of the mouth of God.

Moses continues with another word of testimony. God's providence was remarkable in caring for them.

> Thy raiment waxed not old upon thee, neither did thy foot swell, these forty years. Thou shalt also consider in thine heart, that, as a man chasteneth his son, so the Lord thy God chasteneth thee. Therefore thou shalt keep the commandments of the Lord thy God, to walk in his ways, and to fear him (Deut. 8:4–6).

How can you have the faith and the assurance to walk forward, closer to God, than you have been before? Think back and remember the way He led you. He has been with you and is now watching over you. When it was necessary for Him to chasten you He did it in such a way that it was always helpful. "Therefore thou shalt keep the commandments of the Lord thy God, to walk in his ways, and to fear him."

AND BE YE THANKFUL
(Deuteronomy 8:10–20)

Have you ever realized how important it is to be thankful?

As we look at the Book of Deuteronomy we can see that the things that happened to Israel were written about as examples for our admonition. This Word of God will help believers come closer to the Lord.

Moses continues to instruct the people to be prepared to be thankful to God. He points out to them what a wonderful land has been given to them and urges them to thank God—not themselves—for what He has done for them.

> When thou hast eaten and art full, then thou shalt bless the Lord thy God for the good land which he hath given thee. Beware that thou forget not the Lord thy God, in not keeping his commandments, and his judgments, and his statutes, which I command thee this day (Deut. 8:10–11).

Moses listed some ways in which one could forget God. He was not talking about momentary distraction but rather an attitude where a person leaves God out of his thinking. Moses explained more fully what he meant:

> Lest when thou hast eaten and art full, and hast built goodly houses, and dwelt therein; and when thy herds and thy flocks multiply, and thy silver and thy gold is multiplied, and all that thou hast is multiplied; then thine heart be lifted up, and thou forget the Lord thy God, which brought thee forth out of the land of Egypt, from the house of bondage (Deut. 8:12–14).

After they had eaten the food and were satisfied, after they had built good houses and dwelt in them, after their herds and flocks had multiplied and their silver and gold had increased, then their hearts might be lifted up and they would forget the Lord their God. Note how Moses refers to the Lord their God: he didn't say He was the God who caused their flocks and herds to increase, or the God who caused their crops to mature that they might have a good harvest; Moses called God the One who brought them forth out of the land of Egypt from the house of bondage. Moses warns the Hebrews not to become self-satisfied and proud, forgetting the God who redeemed them from the land of Pharaoh.

The most important thing about a believer's spiritual experience is that Christ Jesus died for him on Calvary's cross, that he has been forgiven his sins, and that God gave His Son to die for him. And these are the simple truths a believer is in grave danger of forgetting.

> And thou say in thine heart, My power and the might of mine hand hath gotten me this wealth (Deut. 8:17).

In his lifetime a believer will receive certain blessings. To whom will he give the credit? If he does not give God the glory and does not turn his heart to Him and thank Him, he will begin to think that he did it. That serious mistake will lead him away from Almighty God.

> But thou shalt remember the Lord thy God: for it is he that giveth thee power to get wealth, that he may establish his covenant which he sware unto thy fathers, as it is this day (Deut. 8:18).

Some people maintain they worked for their wealth, but who

gave them the strength to work? The Lord gives the power to get the wealth that He may establish His covenant with His people.

Moses solemnly warns:

> And it shall be, if thou do at all forget the Lord thy God, and walk after other gods, and serve them, and worship them, I testify against you this day that ye shall surely perish (Deut. 8:19).

We should take this message to heart if we expect to move forward and live closer to God.

BE NOT PROUD IN YOUR OWN CONCEIT
(Deuteronomy 9:1–6)

Did you know that being prosperous is not a sign that your way of doing things is approved by God?

Deuteronomy was written for our learning, and so we look for things that will help us. In our last study we saw how Moses urged the people to be thankful for benefits received, because thanks belongs to God. Otherwise one gives himself the glory. The failure to see God's hand in good fortune causes people to become proud, as we can see in Israel's case. One reason many of us are not closer to God than we are now is because we are too proud of ourselves. Pride is especially a danger to people who are greatly blessed of God. If a person is having a great deal of trouble in life, he is likely to be humbled by events. He may be angry or rebellious, but not proud. But if someone is coming along fine he is inclined to think he is the source of his success.

Moses told the people:

> Hear, O Israel: Thou art to pass over Jordan this day, to go in to possess nations greater and mightier than thyself, cities great and fenced up to heaven, a people great and tall . . . Understand therefore this day, that the Lord thy God is he which goeth over before thee; as a consuming fire he shall destroy them, and he shall bring them down before thy face: so shalt thou drive them out, and destroy them quickly, as the Lord hath said unto thee (Deut. 9:1-3).

Israel will overcome these great and tall people because God will be with the Hebrews. The message for us here is that after we seek God by praying and reading our Bibles, and He does answer, we must be careful to remember that it is God—not us—who gives the victory in answer to prayer. We may think that God blesses us because we are good and acting right, but that does not follow, for many righteous people have trials.

> Speak not thou in thine heart, after that the Lord thy God hath cast them out from before thee, saying, For my righteousness the Lord hath brought me in to possess this land: but for the wickedness of these nations the Lord doth drive them out from before thee. Not for thy righteousness, or for the uprightness of thine heart, dost thou go to possess their land: but for the wickedness of these nations the Lord thy God doth drive them out from before thee, and that he may perform the word which the Lord sware unto thy fathers, Abraham, Isaac, and Jacob (Deut. 9:4–5).

Israel will get the victory, not because they are good, but because the people who are being defeated are so wicked God has to destroy them.

> Understand therefore, that the Lord thy God giveth thee not this good land to possess it for thy righteousness; for thou art a stiffnecked people (Deut. 9:6).

As God looks down on us He knows we are often a stiffnecked people. The word *stiffnecked* refers to oxen. An ox normally works with his head down, and the yoke lies across his shoulders. The ox pushes into the bar with his head in a natural position. But once in awhile an ox becomes aroused and rebellious and throws his head up, in which case the yoke does not fit snugly on his shoulders. Then he is not able to pull a normal load. He is called "stiffnecked" because he does not bow his neck down and fit it into the yoke. Stiffnecked people, then, are rebellious people.

By the grace of God a believer may receive blessing that is far beyond what he deserves. He should be careful not to claim credit for it. By the same token, some may suffer distress that is far heavier than they deserve. The providence of God as it occurs is no proof of what the Lord thinks of us.

REMEMBER YOUR SIN IN THE GOLDEN CALF
(Deuteronomy 9:7–21)

Could anything provoke God to anger?

The gospel tells men of the grace of God by which He will forgive sin. We love to tell the story of Jesus and His love, and those who preach and teach the gospel are glad to tell the whole world that God is long-suffering, plenteous in mercy, slow to anger. But there is another side of the truth: God is the righteous Judge. Paul said, "Behold therefore the goodness and severity of God" (Rom. 11:22).

Men easily get the idea that God will not destroy. I sometimes ask them, "How do you account for death, for destruction of any kind? Are these instances where God has no control?" Many people claim that since God is a God of love, He would never hurt anyone. So when hurt comes it leaves a person with the feeling that God cannot do anything about it. These same people act as if they think they are doing God some honor by saying that He would never punish anybody. However, the Bible does not show a picture of a God who does not judge. The Scriptures actually teach that God is a holy God, of purer eyes than to behold evil, and He is a consuming fire.

Persons who convince themselves that there is no righteous judgment of God deceive themselves. But error in ideas does not change God. God is not so much what I say He is, as He is what He is in Himself, and this is revealed in the Scriptures. We all need to be warned that God will judge sin. Because God is kind and gracious does not mean that He will condone sin.

In order to help Israel come closer to God, Moses reminded them of the truth that was revealed in their own experience when they sinned against God. In Deuteronomy 9:7–21 reference is made to worship of the golden calf. Here Moses is stressing that God actually judged the people at that time. The rebellious conduct of those people in the golden calf incident provoked the Lord to anger. When people know the Lord and then turn away from Him, it provokes God to judgment. Israel was spared only by the faithful and humble intercession of Moses, who stood in the breach and prayed to Almighty God to deliver those who were turning away from Him. They had the wrong idea of God and were worshiping something that was not God. Error in worship, in their concept of God, is forgiven only by intercession.

We should warn one another that the human mind can make mistakes in thinking about God, accumulating ideas that are false according to the Scriptures. When such becomes the case we are in grave danger of offending God. If you know somebody like that you should pray for him. When we think of Moses praying for the children of Israel we feel prompted to pray for our loved ones.

If your heart bothers you because you do not remember to pray all the time, let me tell you something: praying for your people goes on not only in and through you, but our Lord Jesus Christ is praying for us, and for all who put their trust in Him. He is even now in the presence of God, interceding on our behalf. When we remember how Moses interceded on behalf of Israel and was able by his faithfulness in prayer to gain for them a favor from God, so our Lord Jesus Christ is praying for us in the presence of God, seeking to help us. He prays only for those who have turned to and accepted Him.

The realization of our tendency to sin against God is part of the preparation we should make if we want to attain a closer walk with God. Moses pointed out to the Israelites that it was important for them to remember their personal sinfulness, that even when trying to do the will of God they sinned. They should also remember that because somebody prayed for them, they were delivered. In 1 John we are told that if any man see a brother sin a sin which is not unto death he shall ask God to forgive, and He shall give him life.

Moses set an example for us of how becoming humility is to a godly man. This humility is grounded in part in the realization of his own weakness. When praying for others we should be humble, remembering that we were sinners saved by God's grace. We need have no fear, for God is gracious and merciful, and He will not despise a humble and contrite heart.

REMEMBER YOUR SIN AT KADESH-BARNEA
(Deuteronomy 9:22–29)

Would you understand that the more familiar we are with the grace of God, the more we are aware of our sin?

Every now and then we are troubled because some people seem to have no feeling of sin. These ones don't recognize their sin because they aren't seeing the holiness of God. Job in the Old Testament was a very good man. He gave sacrifices to God; he worshiped God and prayed for himself and his family. So far as we know, he tried to do everything right. Yet God allowed Job to suffer severe trials, causing him to lose everything. At the end of his trials Job said:

> I have heard of thee by the hearing of the ear; but now mine eye seeth thee: wherefore I abhor myself, and repent in dust and ashes (Job 42:5–6).

When we become gloriously conscious of His grace and mercy we also become conscious of our sin. So it was with Isaiah when he was in the temple and suddenly saw the glory of God.

> Woe is me! for I am undone; because I am a man of unclean lips, and I dwell in the midst of a people of unclean lips: for mine eyes have seen the King, the Lord of hosts (Isa. 6:5).

Isaiah saw an angel pick up a coal with tongs off the altar and put it on his lips. Then he heard the word coming from God saying to him that his sin was forgiven, his iniquity was cleansed.

We read in the New Testament how Saul the Pharisee became Paul, the apostle. He spoke of himself as being the chief of sinners and again, he spoke of being the least of the saints. As he grew in his knowledge of the Lord Jesus Christ he became more impressed with the weakness of his own human heart.

All the way through the Bible we find that when a man comes into the presence of God he feels himself to be a sinner. Yet while he sees himself as a sinner, the believer sees the Lord Jesus Christ as a Savior. The believer has the promise that "though your sins be as scarlet, they shall be as white as snow; though they be red like crimson, they shall be as wool"(Isa. 1:18), for "where sin abounded, grace did much more abound" (Rom. 5:20). God is calling us to go where people yesterday failed to go; we can draw nearer to God than people did yesterday. We need instruction and guidance on how this can be done, and this we find in Deuteronomy.

Moses had been seeking to reduce the danger of pride in the children of Israel by reminding them of things they had done wrong.

> . . . ye provoked the Lord to wrath. Likewise when the Lord sent you from Kadesh-barnea, saying, Go up and possess the land which I have given you; then ye rebelled against the commandment of the Lord your God, and ye believed him not, nor hearkened to his voice. Ye have been rebellious against the Lord from the day that I knew you (Deut. 9:22–24).

Moses tried to prepare them for entering the land by having them recognize their sin in not coming closer to God. Suppose that today we turn to the Lord and say, "Lord, I want to walk with thee." That would be a proper prayer. "I want to walk closer to thee than I have ever walked before," would also be a proper prayer. But we should have prayed that yesterday or the day before. Let's confess now before the Lord, saying, "Lord, I have been negligent. All the time I should have been walking closer to thee." After confessing this slackness let us ask the Lord to help us.

CHAPTERS 10–12

† † †

HUMBLY TRUST GOD
(Deuteronomy 10)

Do you realize that belonging to God is a privilege?

Every human being created in the image of God is expected to act the way God would want him to act. If he does not do that he will be judged a sinner in the sight of God, and God will deal with him accordingly. The gospel of the Lord Jesus Christ reveals that God has provided a way of salvation through His Son, the Lord Jesus Christ. When a soul accepts Jesus Christ as Savior he will be justified by the free grace of God. After a person has accepted the Lord Jesus Christ and so belongs to God through the Lord Jesus Christ, he can grow in grace and knowledge, learning the ways of God. The word for this is *sanctification*, being separated unto God. Sanctification is only by the free grace of God.

When a believer is so yielded Almighty God lives in him, and the will of God is being done through him. The Holy Spirit is working in him so that certain results follow. "Herein is my Father glorified, that ye bear much fruit" (John 15:8). Sanctification, like salvation, is given freely; at no time is the believer worthy nor does he ever earn it. We do not have to try to qualify, because we could not do it; God understands that and has provided for us.

In chapter 10 we have a summary of the good things God has done for His people. For example, He gave the Ten Commandments for guidance. Israel would benefit by what God has done. The Lord also called the tribe of Levi to serve as priests. All the other Israelites would be benefited to have these men faithfully perform their function. And in verses 10 and 11 we find the greatest act God did for His people: He hearkened unto intercessory prayer by Moses and restored Israel.

Verses 12 and 13 contain a remarkable statement about what God actually requires of His people:

> And now, Israel, what doth the Lord thy God require of thee, but to fear the Lord thy God, to walk in all his ways, and to love him, and to serve the Lord thy God with all thy heart and with all thy soul, to keep the commandments of the Lord, and his statutes, which I command thee this day for thy good? (Deut. 10:12–13).

Because He loved them and chose them, God wanted Israel to circumcise their hearts, deny themselves, crucify their flesh, and take up their crosses. Moses admonished the Israelites:

> Thou shalt fear the Lord thy God; him shalt thou serve, and to him shalt thou cleave, and swear by his name (Deut. 10:20).

Believers are to turn themselves over to God. This is the proper frame of mind with which a person can advance to higher ground. The Lord wants His people to come nearer to Him, and they can come when they humbly trust Him.

YOU KNOW HIS WAYS ENOUGH TO TRUST HIM
(Deuteronomy 11:1–9)

Do you have confidence in God?

To enter into the fullness of salvation a person must obey the will of God as revealed. The will of God may call for us to meekly accept our situation as it is; it does not always follow that if we do the will of God we must do something spectacular. Actually, the will of God may be revealed to us right in the situation in which we now serve, and His will may call for our meekly accepting that situation. God's will for us is to maintain our personal integrity in the face of all manner of evil. No matter how people around us never go to church, we are to engage in the public worship of God. While others in our homes may never read the Bible or pray at all, it is God's will that we do so.

The will of God is that we do what is right regardless of what other people do. It may be that God's will is that we wait patiently for Him even if we do not know for sure what we wait for. But we will have the fullness of the salvation in Christ Jesus if we yield to and obey the will of God as it is revealed to us. We find these truths here in the Book of Deuteronomy.

The first nine verses of chapter 11 record how Moses showed these people that they had reason for trusting God. Moses knew that if his people were to enter into Canaan they must obey the Lord. He well remembered that the first generation came to Kadesh-Barnea within two years after they left Egypt; but they failed to obey the Lord and thus failed to enter the land. Moses had confidence now in the readiness of the new generation to obey the will of God, for these were people who had experiences with God.

> For I speak not with your children which have not known
> . . . (Deut. 11:2)

Moses was speaking to people who did know God. He pointed out that these people knew about the wonders God had performed in Egypt and the miracles He had worked since; they had reason to trust God. The older people had seen the hand of God in their affairs. Moses concluded:

> But your eyes have seen all the great acts of the Lord which he did. Therefore shall ye keep all the commandments which I command you this day, that ye may be strong, and go in and possess the land, whither ye go to possess it (Deut. 11:7-8).

We are to keep the commandments and think about doing the will of God lest we fail; we are to be strong; and we are to take by faith that which has been promised to us that we may be forever with Him. A good way to prepare for what will bring us closer to the Lord is either previous experience of Him or the experience of other people. All believers who have seen what God has done should be disposed to turn to Him and put their trust in Him. Living the life of self-denial, with yielded obedience to the will of God in everything, will demand on our part full trust and confidence in the promises of God. And that trust and confidence will come as we consider the things God has done.

LIVING IN OBEDIENCE IS DIFFERENT
(Deuteronomy 11:10–17)

Do you realize that living in faith is entirely different from any other kind of living?

"The just shall live by faith" (Heb. 10:38) is one of the famous statements of Scripture. It has been called Martin Luther's text because so much light came into his soul when these words came alive for him. This Scripture can be understood as emphasizing that a person is justified by faith, that a soul comes into the presence of God by faith. It is usually understood to mean that one is saved by believing in the Lord Jesus Christ, not by any of his own works. This verse also means that a believing person lives in faith: the just (he who is already accepted of God) shall live by and through faith.

Living in faith is different from natural living. Until now in our reading Moses has been preparing the children of Israel for going into the land of Canaan, which would be a different experience for them. Our study now brings us to Deuteronomy 11:10–17 where Moses points out the difference in living by faith and living in any other way. He likens this to natural difference in the country of Egypt and the country of Canaan, one of the differences being in the lay of the land.

> For the land, whither thou goest in to possess it, is not as the land of Egypt, from whence ye came out, where thou sowedst thy seed, and wateredst it with thy foot, as a garden of herbs (Deut. 11:10).

In those days men used something like a mill wheel with buckets to catch the water which would revolve on a contraption very much like a treadmill. By using their feet as on a bicycle they would supply power that turned this wheel, and the water would be brought up out of the canal and poured out on the land. The point was that the land of Egypt was irrigated by human invention. Moses said the whole country of Egypt was like that.

> But the land, whither ye go to possess it, is a land of hills and valleys, and drinketh water of the rain of heaven: a land which the Lord thy God cared for: the eyes of the Lord thy God are

> always upon it, from the beginning of the year even unto the
> end of the year (Deut. 11:11–12).

Anyone acquainted with irrigation knows that a field filled
with hills and valleys could not be irrigated; it must be watered by rain from heaven. And just the same, there is a big
difference between living by our own works or living by
trusting in God.

Living by our own works would be like irrigating our own
fields with a treadmill. Many are seeking to do that every day.
In the natural world the promotion of results is by works: we
scheme, work, plan, push, and pull to make things happen. In
the spiritual world the promotion of results is by faith in God
who will do more for us than we can ask or think. Egypt could
be irrigated by human devices, but Canaan could not. Canaan
depends only upon God and His blessing.

In the spiritual world blessing comes directly from God,
and will not be sent from God when there is disobedience.
This is what Moses was driving home to them. The great
difference was between living in obedience to God and depending upon Him, and living in their own strength which
could result in barren, unfruitful failure.

Believers are not always perfect, and when we make mistakes we confess them. When there is something wrong about
us we ask God to forgive us. We are glad to remember that
the blood of the Lord Jesus Christ cleanses us from all sin. But
we know that blessing is directly dependent upon our faith in
God. We know that if we have unbelief in our hearts we will
not be able to serve Him in spiritual matters. Living in obedience to the will of God in the Holy Spirit is quite different
from living in the natural world.

OBEDIENCE BRINGS BLESSING
(Deuteronomy 11:18–32)

Do you know what one thing is necessary for a person to live a
consecrated life?

Living in fellowship with the Lord is really not a complicated matter. We talk about it, because it is so important, and we know that many really wish to live closer to Him. Some do not come closer because they do not fully understand how. Being a believer is not primarily a matter of morals; some unbelievers live right morally, while some believers have a hard time doing that which is right. Living as a believer is a matter of living in yielded obedience to the living God.

Paul writes: "And whatsoever ye do in word or deed, do all in the name of the Lord Jesus" (Col. 3:17). The particular situation you are in will leave you something to do. What you do at any given time is largely determined by the situation and the time you are living in. But when you do move forward in all good conscience what is your motivation? This is the point where the Gospel applies. Jesus of Nazareth said, "I do all things to please my Father" (John 8:29). He did not do things primarily to make money or to please His neighbors or because society thought it was a good thing. He had a personal relationship with His Father, and this is what guided Him. On another occasion He said, "I do nothing of myself. My Father worketh hitherto and I work" (John 5:17).

Living a spiritual life means that a person acts in his normal manner, but he does so as unto the Lord. If a person does the routine things as a believer, as unto the Lord, the Lord will strengthen him and bless him. Others will see what happens and be benefitted. The believer does not act primarily on account of other people; he does what he does because he wants to do what is pleasing in the sight of the Lord. A believer is not necessarily spiritual because he prays, or because he reads the Bible. Some of the most cantankerous people in the world read the Bible. A believer is spiritual when he is being moved by the Holy Spirit, when he does whatever he does in obedience to Him.

Moses made all this plain in his summary at this point in Deuteronomy.

> Therefore shall ye lay up these my words in your heart and in your soul, and bind them for a sign upon your hand, that they may be as frontlets between your eyes. And ye shall teach them your children, speaking of them when thou sittest in thine house, and when thou walkest by the way, when thou

liest down, and when thou risest up. And thou shalt write
them upon the door posts of thine house, and upon thy gates:
that your days may be multiplied, and the days of your children, in the land which the Lord sware unto your fathers to
give them, as the days of heaven upon the earth (Deut. 11:
18–21).

In our day the important thing for the believer to do is to read
the Bible, and when he has opportunity, to share it with
others. Even if he cannot always read the Bible, he can be
yielded in his mind and heart to the Lord. The Holy Spirit
will be given to him to bring the things of God to his heart and
mind.

Moses gave the promise of victory over alien forces:

For if ye shall diligently keep all these commandments which
I command you, to do them, to love the Lord your God, to
walk in all his ways, and to cleave unto him; then will the
Lord drive out all these nations from before you, and ye shall
possess greater nations and mightier than yourselves (Deut.
11:22–23).

The believer can have constant victory if he will keep the
Word of God in his heart. Moses added a marvelous promise:

Every place whereon the soles of your feet shall tread shall be
yours: from the wilderness and Lebanon, from the river, the
river Euphrates, even unto the uttermost sea shall your coast
be (Deut. 11:24).

This truth has reference to the promises of God. There is
great assurance in the promise, "There shall no man be able to
stand before you" (Deut. 11:25).

Verses 26 to 28 give us a decision to make: "Behold, I set
before you this day a blessing and a curse" (Deut. 11:26).
The Hebrews could be either with God and have His favor,
or they could be without Him and be cursed. Yielded obedience to the revealed will of God is the way to blessing. If a
believer wants to draw nigh unto God, and if he wants his
spiritual life to be strong and fruitful, there is one thing that
is necessary: he must know the Word of God and must respond to it.

BE CAREFUL IN WORSHIP
(Deuteronomy 12)

Does it make any difference what a man thinks about when he goes to church?

Beginning with chapter 12 the record shows that Moses becomes more specific in giving instruction. Moses, in preparing the Israelites for entry into Canaan, urges them to think about certain matters. To begin with he lays emphasis upon the public worship of God. From the beginning and through today this topic has had the utmost significance. For example, when the wise men from the east found the Christ child they first worshiped Him; after that they presented their gifts.

We could raise the question, "Isn't it enough to go to church? Does it matter what one thinks, and would not one church be as good as another?" Moses would say that you should be very careful about how you worship God. He told Israel in chapter 12 to completely destroy everything the former inhabitants had used in worshiping their gods.

> Ye shall utterly destroy all the places, wherein the nations which ye shall possess served their gods, upon the high mountains, and upon the hills, and under every green tree: and ye shall overthrow their altars, and break their pillars, and burn their groves with fire; and ye shall hew down the graven images of their gods, and destroy the names of them out of that place (Deut. 12:2-3).

There are all kinds of false worship in the world. Some pagans worship manmade objects and their elaborate shrines. Some follow certain sacred rites such as saying a prayer over and over, the more times the better. Some church organizations promote certain false ideas by a sort of planned propaganda. These things men call worship.

But Moses would say that if a believer wants to walk with God and have close fellowship with Him he would have to utterly destroy all these pagan practices. Moses instructed the Hebrews to worship at the place which God had chosen. For us that would be the foot of the cross of Calvary where we can look into the face of Jesus Christ that we might look into the face of God. The worshiper is not to do whatever is right in his own eyes, he is to do what God wants him to do. He should come into the presence of God and bow down before Him. Moses instructed the Hebrews to be very careful to have the right attitude and actions. Today a worshiper should come to church to find out about the Lord Jesus Christ.

When a believer goes to church he meets God, and this meeting does not depend on the building, the choir, or on the other people who are there. The worshiper should think about the Lord Jesus Christ dying for him. This is the very essence of acceptable worship.

> Take heed to thyself that thou be not snared by following them. . . . Thou shalt not do so unto the Lord thy God. . . . What thing soever I command you, observe to do it: thou shalt not add thereto, nor diminish from it (Deut. 12:30–32).

God is very much concerned that the believer should come before Him humbly, simply and honestly, and look into the face of Jesus Christ, where he will see the glory of Almighty God. Doing this will promote his personal spiritual experience.

CHAPTERS 13–18

† † †

LET NO MAN DECEIVE YOU
(Deuteronomy 13)

Do you know there are imitations of the gospel being preached that seek to win your endorsement?

Spiritual living is complicated by unsound preaching. Human beings do not know much about the things of heaven. Men live in this world, and God is invisible, heaven is invisible, and spiritual things are invisible. God has intended that believers should learn of the spiritual from those who know. Thus the truth comes by preaching: "It pleased God by the foolishness of preaching to save them that believe" (1 Cor. 1:21). "So then faith cometh by hearing, and hearing by the word of God" (Rom. 10:17).

We listen to learn. When we hear someone preach who has ideas different from our own, we caution ourselves to be tolerant lest we judge him unjustly. But we must know the Word of God well enough to know where to draw the line on listening to others, or before we know it, our hearts and minds will be open to any doctrine.

It is easy to be impressed by an orator who has a fancy flow of words; it is also easy to be impressed by a faker, or a spell-binder. Perhaps the most dangerous of all is the man who really carries out his false ideas.

Chapter 13 of Deuteronomy should be read time and time again. Moses gave the children of Israel definite guidance as to whom they should listen to and follow. Perhaps there is no one more susceptible to following error, than an eager soul who wants to draw near to God. One almost wonders why it should be that way, yet it happens many times. An inexperienced listener may not be able to discern whether the message such a false prophet brings is right or wrong. Many naïve young people go to college and listen to some professor presenting his subject in such a way as to put down God's Word, and they cannot find anything wrong with what he says. An experienced person might detect the weakness in the argument, and try to stop the man and point out his weakness. But the professor can spin his tale before the people and guide them along in his way of thinking past spots, where some may have pointed out he was wrong but others could not see it. Weak believers may believe the man's false teaching and fall away from God, no longer wanting to go to church, read the Bible, or pray. They feel these things do not count.

Moses sought to impress upon the people the fact that they had been committed to the Lord by their deliverance. In a similar way believers have been redeemed by the blood of the Lord Jesus Christ. God may allow these dreamers of dreams to present spurious ideas and false notions to test His people, to see whether they really love the Lord their God with all their heart and all their soul and all their might. It was to guard against such peril that Paul wrote:

> But continue thou in the things which thou hast learned and hast been assured of, knowing of whom thou hast learned them; and that from a child thou hast known the holy scriptures, which are able to make thee wise unto salvation through faith which is in Christ Jesus (2 Tim. 3:14–15).

Moses does not present a big argument to prove all others are wrong; he presents no in-depth discussion and analysis to show the weakness of other leaders. In Isaiah's time also there were false prophets. The revelation of the truth was dimmer in those days than it was in New Testament times, but even then there were people who came and offered things that would mislead. Isaiah said,

> To the law and to the testimony: if they speak not according to this word, it is because there is no light in them (Isa. 8:20).

In Joshua 9 we read that the great soldier Joshua was completely fooled by certain people who came to him and pretended to be something other than what they were. When we read that closely we find that Joshua "inquired not at the mouth of the Lord." He took these men at their own evaluation. They said they were good men, and Joshua accepted it that way and made a mistake. He got the whole country into trouble because he was not careful.

God permits such deceivers to test a believer's fidelity. Moses warned that some may come from one's own family. Action against such persons was to be severe. In our time with our laws and culture being as they are, believers cannot do anything to punish false prophets, but each believer can do something about them in his own heart and mind. Believers must treat false prophets just as they would treat a person who brings smallpox into their homes. Each believer must take heed that no man deceives him; he must take his stand by the cross of Calvary.

REFRAIN FROM WORLDLY PRACTICES
(Deuteronomy 14)

Do you expect to see any difference between believers and unbelievers?

To have the fullness of the blessing of salvation a believer must walk with the Lord, trusting him to help in everyday affairs. Do you think that walking with Christ can be entirely private? Should a believer keep his relationship with the Lord secret?

Should the gospel be shown to the world? Paul said, "If our gospel be hid, it is hid to them that are lost" (2 Cor. 4:3). Almighty God, through the Lord Jesus Christ, is interested in the people of the world. He would like to win them to Himself, and the only way is for the gospel to be presented through those who do believe. The Lord Jesus said to His disciples, "You shall be witnesses unto me" (Acts 1:8). A witness does not keep quiet; he tells the facts openly. Paul also said to the Corinthians, "Forasmuch as ye are manifestly declared to be the epistle of Christ ministered by us" (2 Cor. 3:3). If we are the epistle of Christ (a letter, as it were), our lives are to be read. And if a believer is to enter into the fullness of the blessing that is in Christ Jesus, it will be important for him to openly identify himself with Christ.

Moses gave specific instructions for the people of Israel to conduct themselves differently than others.

> Ye are the children of the Lord your God: ye shall not cut yourselves, nor make any baldness between your eyes for the dead (Deut. 14:1).

Now you and I may wonder what he meant. The idea is this: in those days, among the Canaanites, there was a common practice in lamenting for the dead that mourners cut their flesh and shaved their heads between the eyes. Moses gave definite instructions to the people of Israel that they were not to conform to such practices of pagan people; Israel was to belong to God in a special way.

> For thou art a holy people unto the Lord thy God, and the Lord hath chosen thee to be a peculiar people unto himself, above all the nations that are upon the earth (Deut. 14:2).

The word *holy* comes from the English word *whole,* meaning "altogether." Israel was to be altogether given over to serve the Lord. When the King James Version says they were "peculiar," it does not mean they were "funny," but that they had distinctive character and belonged to God in a special way.

Beginning with the third verse the record shows they were to be careful about their diet. Some foods were unclean and were not to be eaten. In many cases modern scientific judgment concurs with these Old Testament designations so that today their choice of these foods for health reasons would be largely endorsed. However when we take this particular Scripture to ourselves it means far more than the physical food that we would eat. We should consider what our intellectual and spiritual diets are. Materials available for their food contained certain elements that were unclean; just as intellectual material in our day and time has some elements in it that are unclean.

On the public market today, things are sold that are not clean. A believer in Christ could be recognized by the fact that he makes no use of unclean literature, unclean movies, or unclean philosophies. These all promote popular worldly concepts, which must be rejected by believers. We should take heed of what we hear and see just as the Hebrews were to

take heed of what they ate, and we should do this because we
belong to God in a special way.

In the latter part of this chapter Moses talks about tithing.
The children of Israel were to bring their tithe, and eat it
before the Lord. Here again is a practice we know very little
about. It would seem they took some of the money that had
been given to the Levites, and used it in a way that had
religious significance. They were to come specifically to the
place where the name of the Lord was set forth. And they
were to do this in a way that would show they were receiving
this blessing from God.

The Hebrews were also given instruction that the Levite
was not to be forsaken. Respect for the ministry is also a
witness to the Lord. Any person who wants to be a strong
believer will be very careful to support those who are minis-
tering the gospel. Ample support of the ministry is a witness
of true faith. Every three years the Hebrews were to distrib-
ute the tithe, and the Levites, strangers, orphans, and widows
were to be provided for in it.

BE LIBERAL IN CHARITY
(Deuteronomy 15)

Would you expect a believer to be charitable?

Walking close to the Lord makes a difference in anybody's
life. Some feel this difference should be seen in the way they
act. Some people, in their zeal to show they are different,
refrain from going to certain places and doing certain things,
and in a great many cases their faithfulness has a definite
influence among their friends and relatives, and in the community in which they live.

Some people try to show this difference in their clothing.
We respect people like that. God looks on the heart, but
when a sincere believer wants to please God and does it by
dressing in a certain fashion I am sure the Lord understands.
Yet there is a more profound way in which we can show the
difference between believers and unbelievers.

In Deuteronomy 15, Moses indicated to the children of Israel that when they went into the land and lived in the blessing of God, they were to be careful to act differently from others, with reference to the poor. In verses 1–18 an interesting sketch is given of the way the children of Israel were to deal with the poor. It is written that "at the end of every seven years thou shalt make a release." This seems to mean they were to cancel debts with other Hebrews, yet they still could collect their money from foreigners.

There are so many different people in the world we cannot deal with everybody as if we all belonged to the same family. However, we could do that with the people who are in our own church, with people who are related, spiritually speaking. Moses told his people when they went into the land of Canaan they were to treat each other with special concern.

Every now and again the possibility of cancelling debts is discussed. Some of the inspiration undoubtedly stems from this portion of Scripture. Perhaps some think such a practice would be good economically. I do not think Moses did it here to promote good economics. He did think the Lord would bless them, but he was doing this because it indicated that God's people should treat each other like brethren.

In this portion we read that the poor will always be in the land, and the children of Israel will have to take care of them. Every seven years they were to cancel all debts and let the poor start over again. Some say such a procedure is not fair, but I am not sure Moses was doing this because it was or was not fair; I think Moses was doing this because it was what God wanted done. It was quite obviously practical. Nobody would get hurt this way. If one man had the ability to make and save money, and he loaned it to a man who had no money because this man was his brother, then at the end of seven years he would cancel the debt because the man could not repay it.

Moses called it wicked if a man should deny a brother money, realizing that it was the fifth year, so that in two years that debt would be cancelled. The principle involved is brethren, in dealing with each other, should not do so with the idea of making money out of each other; they should do so with the idea of helping one another. In this way they would be different from other people. Moses spoke plainly to say that refusal to help the poor brother "will be a sin unto thee."

Moses also dealt with the matter of slavery. In those days slavery was being under contract for the rest of your life. But Moses laid down the rule that if the slave were a brother, at the end of the seven years he should go free, and when freed he should be given a bonus.

Moses also had something to say about dealing with the increase of the flocks and herds. When the first male would be born, it was to be set aside unto God. In this way God would be recognized as the giver of every increase. If this male was without blemish, it was to be given to God to bring Him honor.

The real difference between Israel and other nations appeared in the way they managed their affairs. A person can be different in appearance by cutting his hair a certain way or by wearing a certain uniform, or by doing certain things, but the real difference between people is in their conduct. Their charity among themselves as brethren will distinguish them. We can understand the importance of the New Testament word:

> And above all things have fervent charity among yourselves (1 Peter 4:8).

It is always impressive when believing people in a congregation treat each other like brethren. Nothing scandalizes the world as much as a church quarrel. But when the people in the church are friendly and brotherly toward one another, this is a blessing to everybody.

REFRAIN FROM WORLDLY PRACTICES IN PUBLIC WORSHIP
(Deuteronomy 16)

Is it important for a believer to join in public worship?

Consecrated living is definitely a matter of heart attitude. If a person really wants to come near to God he will have to have a hunger deep down inside his soul. Walking with the Lord is a matter of inward commitment, yet participation in public worship is vital. What a man does openly affects him inwardly. A person can have feelings inside, but if he never expresses them in any way they will get weaker. On the other hand, if a person has feelings in his heart and expresses them in some way they will become stronger.

We know that agricultural crops prosper by being tended, and children grow up and become intelligent by being schooled. The same is true spiritually, and Moses wanted the Israelites to be persistent in their intention to walk with God. So in Deuteronomy 16 he instructed them to participate in certain public religious exercises.

First, the Israelites were to remember their deliverance from Egypt and to participate in the Passover Feast. They were to hold this feast in the place in which the Lord "shall choose to place His name there." This expression is used a number of times in Deuteronomy; it referred to a particular designated spot where God would lead them in order to manifest Himself. You and I can have this in mind for today. I am persuaded that the one place where God has determined to put His name is at the cross of Calvary. When I look at that I know I am face to face with God.

When we think of the Passover Feast we are reminded of a common practice among believers that points directly to the same truth. The Lord's Supper is among Christian people what the Passover Feast was among the people of Israel. In the Passover Feast the Hebrews remembered how the lamb was slain and how they were spared; in the Lord's Supper we remember how Christ Jesus died for us and how through His dying we are spared. In partaking of the Lord's Supper at such times, as we break the bread and drink the cup, we should emphasize the presence of the Lord Jesus Christ. The actual eating of the bread and the drinking of the cup will have no special value to the believer unless he is conscious of the fact that the Lord Jesus Christ was Himself involved. The worshiper should seek some personal consciousness of the Lord's presence with him at that time.

After the Passover Feast Scripture describes a feast of weeks that seems to be very much like Pentecost. Seven weeks (forty-nine days) after the offering of the firstfruits they were to celebrate. That would be fifty days of Pentecost. When the harvest was complete, they were to publicly have this feast of weeks and to bring a freewill offering in their hands to God, and to rejoice. Then they were given instructions to hold another feast—the Feast of Tabernacles for seven days which they were to celebrate because of harvest. There was to be praise and thanksgiving with joy. Here they again brought gifts and shared them lavishly before the Lord with joy and thanksgiving because God had been good to them. This could be the origin of the New Testament statement, "God loveth a cheerful giver" (II Cor. 9:7b). If you have had friends who are real believers and have entered into a full understanding of the gospel, you will know people who have great joy in bringing their own money to give to the Lord.

Three times a year all the men were to present themselves before God and make a freewill offering. It was a kind of roll call of all the men who came in thankfulness to give to the Lord. Each was to give according to the abundance of blessing of the Lord. We have noted four different activities these people were to perform, each of which would remind them of certain benefits. When they all did it together they would think more about it than they would when they were alone.

> Thou shalt not plant thee a grove of any trees near unto the altar of the Lord thy God, which thou shalt make thee. Neither shalt thou set thee up any image; which the Lord thy God hateth (Deut. 16:21–22).

In those days the grove was the place of pagan amusement. The Hebrews were not to bring worldly pleasure into the place of worship. We should have real concern about the way our churches are being conducted in these days; when a man comes into the presence of God he should come with the idea of worship.

"Neither shalt thou set thee up any image." The image was a pagan idol. The children of Israel were to have no pagan idols or thoughts when they came to worship God. They were not to give themselves over to natural thinking when they came into the presence of God; they were not to act like the people around them in the building of groves and the setting up of images.

ADMINISTRATION OF DISCIPLINE
(Deuteronomy 17)

Would a really consecrated Christian ever break off fellowship with anyone else?

In the days of the Book of Deuteronomy, Moses instructed the people in many ways to do the will of God and kept telling them to remember what he said. In our day the Holy Spirit helps us with these matters. What Moses wrote will help us to understand what the Spirit will prompt us to do, and the Holy Spirit will move us to do the things He has in mind. In chapter 17 Moses instructs the people to check their conduct carefully. Here he deals with the administration of discipline. He tells them plainly about sacrifices.

> Thou shalt not sacrifice unto the Lord thy God any bullock, or sheep, wherein is blemish, or any evil-favouredness: for that is an abomination unto the Lord thy God (Deut. 17:1).

They were not to bring any inferior gifts to the Lord, only the best. When Mary anointed the Lord Jesus she brought the precious box of spikenard, the very best she had. This shows reverence to God.

> If there be found among you, within any of thy gates which the Lord thy God giveth thee, man or woman, that hath wrought wickedness in the sight of the Lord thy God, in transgressing his covenant, and hath gone and served other gods, and worshipped them, either the sun, or moon, or any of the host of heaven, which I have not commanded; and it be told thee, and thou hast heard of it, and inquired diligently, and behold, it be true, and the thing certain, that such abomination is wrought in Israel (Deut. 17:2-4).

If an accusation was made by only one person they were not to do anything about it. But if it were established in the mouth of two or more witnesses that a person actually turned away from the things of the Lord and began to worship gods of the people round about, he was to be destroyed. This may seem very stern—as stern as it would be to amputate your foot because your foot is diseased and you want to stay alive. If anyone really wants to grow in spiritual matters he must be prepared to repudiate anything that dishonors God. In our day, the laws being what they are, there is no danger of anybody being put to death for such acts of disobedience, but we must no longer count those who worship other gods as belonging with us, as belonging to the Lord. Such repudiation must be done to save the group as a whole.

If one person were to ask another to judge between two people, and he did not know what he should do, he could go to the priest and so get an authorized person to tell him what the Lord would say. Thus he could seek guidance from God about the problem, but he must obey whatever was revealed. If a person did not obey, Moses would call that presumptuous disregard of responsible guidance. Then out of respect for the people who do follow God and out of respect for the man who told the truth, the people were to destroy this person.

You may ask yourself what that means for us in our day and time. We do not stone such offenders today; so what can we do? We must not become involved with them. Moses predicted the day would come when the people would ask for a king. He then distinctly tells them that when the people do ask for a king they should get a good king who will follow the Word of God. The king should keep the Word before him at all times in order to be sure he finds out what God wants him to do.

Each believer has been made a king to serve God, to carry out God's will. Just as Moses gave instructions for kings to be careful about the Word of God, so is every believer today to obey in just that way. The apostle Paul, after having preached to others, did not want himself to be a castaway, and so he wrote, "But I keep under my body, and bring it into subjection." This is what the king must do.

The man who will walk with the Lord must control himself in righteousness. He must show reverence toward God and respect toward other people, and he must fulfill his responsibility.

DEALING WITH PREACHERS
(Deuteronomy 18)

Do you think a preacher is someone special?

Walking with the Lord is a matter of faith. A person must

first believe in Him. If anyone wants to walk closer to God he must have more faith in Him. Normally "faith cometh by hearing [that is, by preaching], and hearing by the Word of God." Paul wrote that it pleased God by the foolishness of preaching to save them that believe.

Moses gave definite instructions about how the people of Israel should act towards the preachers (whom they called Levites) when they entered into the land.

> The priests the Levites, and all the tribe of Levi, shall have no part nor inheritance with Israel: they shall eat the offerings of the Lord made by fire, and his inheritance. Therefore shall they have no inheritance among their brethren: the Lord is their inheritance, as he hath said unto them (Deut. 18:1–2).

This kind of arrangement where the preacher does not own any property or make any living from business is humbling to the preacher and challenging to the believers.

The Levites were to be supplied by the believers.

> And this shall be the priest's due from the people, from them that offer a sacrifice, whether it be ox or sheep (Deut. 18:3).

Moses then told specifically what parts of the animal were to be given to them.

> The firstfruit also of thy corn, of thy wine, and of thine oil, and the first of the fleece of thy sheep, shalt thou give him. For the Lord thy God hath chosen him out of all thy tribes, to stand to minister in the name of the Lord, him and his sons for ever (Deut. 18:4–5).

It has always been God's intention that a minister of the Word should live by using the people's gifts.

Any Levite from any part of Israel would share equally with any other.

> And if a Levite come from any of thy gates out of all Israel, where he sojourned, and come with all the desire of his mind unto the place which the Lord shall choose; then he shall minister in the name of the Lord his God, as all his brethren the Levites do, which stand there before the Lord. They shall have like portions to eat, beside that which cometh of the sale of his patrimony (Deut. 18:6–8).

Moses gave solemn warning against any Levite adopting pagan customs in his family life.

> When thou art come into the land which the Lord thy God giveth thee, thou shalt not learn to do after the abominations of those nations. There shall not be found among you any one that maketh his son or his daughter to pass through the fire, or that useth divination, or an observer of times, or an enchanter, or a witch, or a charmer, or a consulter with familiar spirits, or a wizard, or a necromancer (Deut. 18:9-11).

Despite the most careful guidance and warning by Moses there was unsound leadership in religious practices. The people were often led to do strange things in the name of religion.

> For all that do these things are an abomination unto the Lord: and because of these abominations the Lord thy God doth drive them out from before thee. Thou shalt be perfect with the Lord thy God. For these nations, which thou shalt possess, hearkened unto observers of times, and unto diviners: but as for thee, the Lord thy God hath not suffered thee so to do (Deut. 18:12–14).

While believers should help those who minister the Word of God to them, they should be very careful not to follow those who would lead them into extravagances of one kind or another. Assuring the people that sound leadership would one day be provided, Moses gave an Old Testament picture of the Lord Jesus Christ.

> The Lord thy God will raise up unto thee a Prophet from the midst of thee, of thy brethren, like unto me; unto him ye shall hearken; according to all that thou desiredst of the Lord thy God in Horeb in the day of the assembly, saying, Let me not hear again the voice of the Lord my God, neither let me see this great fire any more, that I die not. And the Lord said unto me, They have well spoken that which they have spoken. I will raise them up a Prophet from among their brethren, like unto thee, and will put my words in his mouth; and he shall speak unto them all that I shall command him (Deut. 18:15–18).

God would send a Prophet—the Lord Jesus Christ—from among the brethren who would be the one to whom they should listen.

In spite of all the instruction Moses gave there were still men presumptuously preaching their own ideas. This goes on in churches today. Any worshiper comes to church with the expectation that the man in the pulpit will tell the truth, and he is prepared to believe him. Unfortunately the man in the pulpit cannot always be trusted. When false preachers of Moses' day led the people away from the things of the Lord, God dealt sternly with them. We must do the same today. On the other hand, we must recognize and support ministers who preach and teach the Word of God in truth.

CHAPTERS 19–23

† † †

ADMINISTERING SOCIAL JUSTICE
(Deuteronomy 19)

Would you expect a consecrated believer to be concerned about what people do to each other in the community in which he lives?

Living in the fullness of the blessing of God will cause a man to care about how others act and get along. In Deuteronomy 19 Moses instructs the new generation to take an interest in the way people live with each other. Moses sheds light on what the modern believer's attitude should be about the community in which he lives. With New Testament Scriptures in our hearts and minds we understand that a believer's home is in heaven. On earth he is a stranger and a pilgrim. As a matter of fact, his particular function in this world is being an ambassador for Christ.

Since the believer lives in this world, yet is a stranger, it is an open question as to how much attention he should pay to what is going on around him. I am not sure the Bible tells the believer very much about what he should do to make the community do what it should, but I do think the Bible tells the believer how he should act in the community and how he should live with other people. In Deuteronomy 19:1–7 Moses outlines a matter that ordinarily you and I would not know anything about: Israel was to set aside three cities as places of refuge where wrong-doers fleeing from avengers could hide and have freedom until their cases had been properly considered.

Not all homicides are murder. The term we use for a man accidentally killing another is *manslaughter*. Moses used the example here of two men who went into the woods to cut trees. As one man was striking at a tree the head of his ax flew off and hit the other man and killed him. Obviously this was accidental. But in the culture of that time, the members of the family of the man who had been killed would take it on themselves to bring justice to pass by killing the man who had killed their kinsman. Such persons would be called "the avengers of blood." Moses arranged that the killer could flee to safety in one of the three cities of refuge. In time it would be safe for this man to come out and take up his normal way of living. The children of Israel were told that when they were successful in the conquest of more of the land, they were to add three more cities of refuge.

The intention of this system was not to forbid punishment in some cases. If there was a case where it was determined that a man actually killed another on purpose and then fled to a city of refuge for safety, the elders of that city should take that man and bring him to the avenger of blood, who would kill him. In this way an attempt was made to see that justice would be done, but there would be charity and protection for the innocent.

> Thou shalt not remove thy neighbour's landmark, which they of old time have set in thine inheritance, which thou shalt inherit in the land that thy Lord thy God giveth thee to possess it (Deut. 19:14).

When the Israelites took the country over they surveyed it and set down certain landmarks to show the limits of each family's property. In time these would become well known landmarks for the entire community. Moses gave explicit instructions that no one was to remove a neighbor's landmark. However cheaters would move the landmarks so they could claim land that otherwise would not be theirs.

In our day land is accurately surveyed, so people don't have to worry about neighbors moving landmarks. But the general principle can be applied to many things; we should not disturb arrangements to which people are accustomed. Another important principle to be noted was that if one man accused another in law, nobody should be condemned by the witness of just one man; "In the mouth of two or three witnesses every word may be established." False witnesses are to be punished.

Moses showed how righteous people should live, so that justice was not abused and the innocent were protected. By adopting such principles there would be fairness and equity throughout the whole of society.

OUR SPIRITUAL WARFARE
(Deuteronomy 20)

Do you think believers fight spiritual wars?

Impressed by the meek humility of Jesus, it is easy to think that Christians should never be involved in conflict. But we are overlooking the conflict Jesus had with Satan in the desert, the conflict He had with the Pharisees, and the conflict He endured in Gethsemane. Those experiences were not merely in Christ's imagination. While He was here on earth He was in direct opposition to forces that were moving to destroy Him.

Calvary was not the end of all war. Such an idea ignores the call of the apostles for believers to wage a good warfare. Paul said, "I have fought a good fight" (2 Tim. 4:7); and "Endure hardness as a good soldier . . . no man that warreth entangleth himself with the affairs of this life" (2 Tim. 2:3–4). On another occasion he wrote, "For we wrestle not against flesh and blood, but against principalities, against powers, against the rulers of the darkness of this world, against spiritual wickedness in high places" (Eph. 6:12). Much of Paul's language seems to indicate that believers are involved in a real and desperate war.

We do not fight with flesh and blood. Consecration to God in Christ Jesus means taking up the battle against rulers of the world, our old nature, and the devil. The weapons of our warfare are not carnal but spiritual, and no man can be blessed in the Lord Jesus Christ apart from victory. When we use the phrase "victorious living," we speak of having victory in Christ. A person will never have a victory if he never has a fight.

For Israel to enter the Promised Land they had to go to

war. They may not have thought of going to battle when they left Egypt. Rather I suspect that when they were called to come out of Egypt, all they had in mind was getting away from the terrible rule of Pharaoh. But God was bringing them into Canaan, a land already full of people, where conflict was inevitable. Moses, therefore, gave them instruction about going to war.

We think not so much of going to war politically and in a military fashion, but of war where spiritual matters are concerned. In spiritual life we find opposition, and at times, as we live to the glory of the Lord Jesus Christ, we have a real fight on our hands. Moses told the Israelites they could go into battle with confidence because the Lord would help them. Believers today who do His will have the same promise.

A person may go into battle right in his own home. The nature of that battle will be with spirits other than the Holy Spirit, possibly causing members of his family to oppose him when he obeys the Lord Jesus Christ. Such a believer can be encouraged as he remembers the words of Moses:

> When thou goest out to battle against thine enemies, and seest horses, and chariots, and a people more than thou, be not afraid of them: for the Lord thy God is with thee, which brought thee up out of the land of Egypt (Deut. 20:1).

As he was preparing the Israelites for battle Moses indicated that if for any reason a man was not wholehearted in his intention to fight the enemy or he was fearful and lacking in courage, he should not engage in the battle. And this is a way of saying that if any believer has misgivings about taking a positive stand for the gospel or has any inclination to shrink from open confession of Jesus Christ, he cannot expect to share in victory with the Lord.

In Deuteronomy 20:10–14 believers are encouraged to seek peace, but if it is not possible then they should expect conflict. The Israelites were instructed to take advantage of the spoil of the cities far away from where they were to settle, but were to completely destroy every living thing in the cities they were to inherit. Moses gave this command for the Hebrews' future protection. Fruit-bearing trees were the only things to be saved, and they also were for the benefit of the Hebrews' future. In his battle with evil the believer must be careful not to jeopardize anything that is needful for life because, after all, he wants to live. He must choose to keep virtues and destroy ungodly habits. Yet when the believer engages in conflict he must not do it in such a way that he will harm himself and others.

These principles will be meaningful as the Holy Spirit applies them in us. When a person thinks of his life as a believer, he should not be deceived; he is at war. But the believer is encouraged when he remembers that he has the Lord God Himself with him.

EQUITY AND JUSTICE
(Deuteronomy 21)

Can a believer live a consecrated life when surrounded by evil?

Life often confronts believers with real trouble in evil circumstances. Moses showed the children of Israel how to act in such a situation. The actual circumstances described in chapter 21 may not ever be duplicated in our day, but we can see in these verses the principle of godly living in times of evil. When a slain man was found lying in a field, those who found him were to accept responsibility to do right. They were to measure the distance from where the man lay to various cities, and the city nearest the man was to take responsibility for his burial and related matters. If prisoners of war were brought in, and a man of Israel felt attracted to a woman prisoner, he could take her as his wife. If he later decided he wanted to put her away he could do this, but Moses declared that each person was to be treated fairly. The man putting away his wife was held responsible for his actions.

This is a way of saying that in an evil situation we are to treat each person fairly whether he is good or bad, right or wrong. We may not have to deal with prisoners of war, but sometimes we must deal with persons of bad reputation. Moses would say with Bible authority that if you are a godly person you will act towards such in a fair manner. In

Deuteronomy 21:15–17 an illustration is given where a man had two wives. In Moses' time that was allowed. Each wife had a son and while the husband preferred the second wife, Moses said he could not take the son of the second wife and place him over the son of the first wife. It was not the fault of the firstborn that he was born into an unfavorable situation. Each person should receive his just due regardless of who his parents were. A person must not treat other people according to his own feelings and prejudices.

In Deuteronomy 21:18-21 another case in point is described. If a man's son is stubborn (we might call him incorrigible), Moses said he was to condemn him even though he was his own son. He and his wife were to bring the rebellious son before the people, and let them condemn him the way they would the son of anyone else. Godly parents can have ungodly children. Eli had sons not worthy of him as did Samuel. But if a person is a genuine believer in the Lord Jesus Christ and he wants to be obedient and useful to Him, he must condemn sin anywhere it is found.

This is part of what it means to live godly in an ungodly situation. The believer must realize that right is right and wrong is wrong regardless of who is involved. Deuteronomy 21:22–23 presents a situation we may never have to face. Moses said that if the people hanged a man for an offense of which he was really guilty, after he was dead, they should take him down and give him a proper burial. Believers today may have to condemn evil and they may have to reject it, but when judgment is done the believer can be charitable and do that which is good. Some believers have to face evil every day and this may place them in difficult situations, but they can live godly by the grace of God.

GENERAL RULES OF MORALITY
(*Deuteronomy 22*)

Should being a believer affect everything a person does?

Consecrated living is often associated in our minds with the better moments we have in church, or sometimes we think of it as the experience of a person who lives in a godly home surrounded by true believers. When some people talk about serving the Lord, they mean they serve in church as a preacher, elder, or teacher—much as it was in the time of Israel when those who served in the temple were the Levites. But all of us are called to serve the Lord in every situation. In recent years I have come to understand more and more that being a believer is living in fellowship with God in daily affairs.

In Deuteronomy 22 we read that Moses talked in detail about many ordinary situations, some of which were unclean. He wanted the Israelites to know that if they were to actually live with the blessing of God they would have to live every moment of every day in the presence of God. Paul would say the same thing: "Whatsoever ye do in word or deed, do all in the name of the Lord Jesus" (Col. 3:17). In this chapter the first situation described is that of finding something that was lost, like the neighbor's ox that had strayed. The finder was to take it home and keep it until the neighbor claimed it. If anything else was found that belonged to the neighbor the finder was to keep it until he could restore it to the neighbor. Thus they were to restore found articles to their owners always. If a man saw an animal fall into a ditch or in any way get hurt, he was to help the owner lift it up again.

Moses also told the people to be careful about the way they dressed.

> The woman shall not wear that which pertaineth unto a man,
> neither shall a man put on a woman's garment: for all that do so
> are abomination unto the Lord thy God (Deut. 22:5).

In our day when we see people dressing in all kinds of ways we may wonder what that Scripture means. Some people believe that women should not wear slacks, and some think a man should be very careful how he dresses; but I do not know whether it is necessary to be so specific in seeking the meaning. I think this Scripture implies there are natural differences between men and women, and a believer will want to be careful to treat men like men and women like women. It seems that acting with propriety is what is involved here. Everyone knows there is a difference between men and women, and a believer will have the good sense to act accordingly.

Verses 6 and 7 discuss yet another topic. If one of the Israelites came across a bird's nest and wanted to take the young birds, he was permitted to take them but he should not take the mother, for she might hatch birds next year. In that way the Israelite would conserve wildlife, showing due regard for others. Something of as little consequence as saving a bird is in the Bible because things as small as that matter in life. This passage also applies to the way a man conducts himself in showing regard for others.

Deuteronomy 22:8 points out that if a person builds a house with a flat roof, where people walking on that roof might fall off, the builder was to put a railing on it. Just think! A safety measure right here in the Bible! Why would this rule be in the Bible? Because it indicates an attitude towards other people. The New Testament tells us that we should love our neighbors as ourselves, and here it is spelled out in little things. We should remember what we are thinking about in this study of Deuteronomy. We are asking ourselves if a believer can live a godly life in this ungodly world. Yes, he can. Throughout this chapter Moses describes a catalog of situations and told the people how to act properly.

COMMUNITY WELFARE
(Deuteronomy 23)

Would being a spiritual believer affect the privacies of a man's life?

The giving of the Ten Commandments could have been recorded in one chapter, yet the Book of Deuteronomy is thirty-four chapters long, containing the law of God for everyday situations. This makes the Old Testament a real help to us today. Moses told the people of Israel that God would dwell in their camp. That is very much like telling believers that God will be in their homes, or in their community, because they are there. God will be anywhere they are. They should serve

Him wherever they are, because serving Him will mean that they do what He wants them to do. He will guide them, and they will obey Him.

Serving God is made simple for us by God having given us the Holy Spirit who brings into our hearts and minds the will of God as expressed in the Old and New Testaments. In Deuteronomy 23 Moses taught the new generation of Israelites who were to enter the land of promise that their private intimate affairs also must be godly. God knows everything. God is interested in every detail of the lives of believers, and because of this each believer should act in a way that is worthy of His presence.

In the first six verses it was stated that some persons were unfit for fellowship with God. The blemishes named here were physical blemishes and would not disqualify anybody today. But there are spiritual blemishes that isolate humans from coming into fellowship with God. Verses 7 and 8 state that persons who were counted unfortunate in the community were to be made welcome in the presence of God. And verse 9 points out that in time of war a person might have an opportunity to do evil, but the believer must refrain. If the believer got into a fight he should not take unfair advantage of his opponent. Verses 10 and 11 make clear that an unclean man should not impose himself in the fellowship of God. He would be unclean if he had unconfessed sin, but if he confessed his sin the blood of the Lord Jesus Christ would cleanse him from all sin. Verses 12 to 14 deal with matters pertaining to personal sanitation. In verses 15 and 16 the Israelites were told to give asylum to the refugee. If anybody is in trouble and comes to a believer, he should give that person help.

Deuteronomy 23 shows that unclean elements are to be kept away, but today believers need not be uneasy about that—the blood of the Lord Jesus Christ can cleanse from all sin. We must not allow the unclean—those who have not received Him—to remain in our fellowship if they are causing others to fall. However if they receive Jesus Christ, they belong.

Believers are not to take usury from a brother; the claim on relationship of brotherhood is greater than gain. Vows are to be kept and no one should impose on a friendship. If someone invites a believer to come to see him, inviting him to go into the garden and eat (as much as he can hold) he should not put fruit in a basket and take it away; he should not impose on goodwill.

The consecrated Christian will always act in every given situation obedient to the Word of God.

CHAPTERS 24–26

† † †

FAMILY AND COMMUNITY CHARITY
(Deuteronomy 24)

How far should a consecrated believer go in being charitable?

Salvation results in better relationships between men. When we become believers we get along better together. Love for others has always been characteristic of a real believer, and when a believer walks close to the Lord, living a consecrated life in true, spiritual yieldedness, he cares about others. "The love of Christ constraineth us" (2 Cor. 5:14). "For ye know the grace of our Lord Jesus Christ, that, though he was rich, yet for your sakes he became poor, that ye through his poverty might be rich" (2 Cor. 8:9).

With us this love of Christ, this inward disposition to do something on behalf of others, is shed abroad in our hearts by the Holy Spirit who generates an inward, massive impulse to help others. Moses pointed this out to the children of Israel as they were about to go into the land. Deuteronomy 24 shows how love looks in actual performance among people. The first four verses bring up something unpleasant: the divorce of husband and wife. Although Moses here gave them rules for their divorces, he did not approve of divorce. Unlike today, in that time the woman was at a disadvantage. Men were not required to support their former wives; they simply sent them away. However the women were allowed to remarry.

Deuteronomy 24:5 records that a newly wedded man was to stay with his bride for a year, not engaging in business or war, that she might be cheered by his presence. This showed that her feelings were to be considered. Deuteronomy 24:6 points out that taking a millstone in pledge is absolutely forbidden. Millstones were used in the daily process of grinding and baking, and to deprive a household of them, would, in effect, be taking their lives. In those days men were sold as slaves, but in verse 7 Moses ruled that if any man should sell another Israelite as a slave, he was to be stoned to death.

Special instructions about avoiding leprosy were given since it was a communicable disease. The Israelites were to remember instructions given in Leviticus and in Numbers, not so much that leprosy was to be cured, as that others were to be protected from it. Deuteronomy 24:10–13 records that if an Israelite were going to lend money to a poor man on the condition that he gave some security or pledge, and this security were in his house, the creditor should not go into the man's house to take that security; he was to let the debtor bring it out to him. The dignity of the borrower was to be respected; he might be poor, but people should treat him with respect. This principle was also operative in the case of the laborer working for wages. If he was poor, his master was to pay him each night as he needed the money.

Deuteronomy 24:16 points out that each sinner has his own responsibility. A father is not responsible for the sins of his son, and a son is not responsible for the sins of his father. An interesting emphasis that justice is to be made sure for the weak is brought out in verses 17 and 18. The stranger, the fatherless, and the widow are to be protected. Verses 19 to 22 specify that if a man were harvesting a field and by chance left a sheaf lying on the ground he was not to return and pick it up, and if he left some fruit on the trees he was not to go back and get it; it was to be left for the poor.

The elemental principle throughout these passages is love for others. "Love thy neighbor" is the second great commandment. The demonstration of that is to be motivated by memory of Israel's own experience of the grace of God.

THE CHRISTIAN'S INTEGRITY
(Deuteronomy 25)

How far should a believer go in being honest?

Salvation brings a man into fellowship with God. When he

has come into this fellowship he can come nearer to God. To be nearer to God means to be more yielded to Him; and that is more than an idea; it is a frame of mind. A person cannot get nearer to God by walking across a room or going into a church. Nearness is an attitude of heart, and we shall be thinking about that just now. I often wonder, when I hear people speak about the Book of Deuteronomy as though it had been written years after the events described took place, whether they have made a study of the book to understand the significance of it. The physical, geographical, and historical experiences of Israel are important, but I am primarily interested in the fact that all the way through the book there is one theme: anyone who wants to live in the will of God must do certain things to fulfill His will.

In the early part of the book we saw that the will of God was revealed in His Word, and in the New Testament this is done even more fully for us by the Holy Spirit. But we should remember the Holy Spirit uses the Bible, interpreting events and works of God for us in ways that are beyond our understanding. In the Old Testament days the truth was set forth by the law and judgments which were given to the people through Moses. What is promised in the New Testament as the consequence of the Holy Spirit being given, was shown in the Old Testament in so many specific words. Israel was given definite instruction how they were to live when they entered into the Promised Land. For us there are definite things we must do if we want to walk nearer to the Lord and to achieve what He has in mind for us, which is our consecration

Now let us turn our attention to chapter 25 where we shall see again that the revealed will of God for the Israelites was total honesty on their part. No one can possibly be obedient who is not honest. I do not think Moses recorded all the problems that came up with reference to honesty; but these give us an idea of the direction in which the mind of the Lord would focus. Two men having a quarrel were to go before the judges to find out who was right. The council was to study the situation and determine fair punishment for the dishonest man.

Verse 4 changes topics. It says, "Thou shalt not muzzle the ox when he treadeth out the corn" (Deut. 25:4). Here Moses may very well have had in mind that the Israelites were to be fair all the way across the board, even to their beasts. Elsewhere in the Bible we are told that the righteous man has regard for the life of his beast.

Deuteronomy 25:5–10 sets forth a rather complicated idea that we are no longer bound by, but there is a principle involved—the principle of protecting the family inheritance. The land was originally divided up and given to the various families, and ownership would pass from father to son. If the father died before the son was born there was a special social arrangement made whereby the dead man's brother was to marry the dead man's wife and bear an heir to hold the title to that piece of property.

A private matter is mentioned in verses 11 and 12, and the message is that unfair tactics will be punished. A practical matter is mentioned in verses 13 to 16, and we do not have any trouble understanding it. The people were told to keep a system of true weights. This principle should be followed today. When anyone sells goods he is to have full sixteen ounces in a pound, thirty-six inches in a yard, and thirty-two ounces in a quart. Dishonesty is an abomination unto the Lord.

Finally, in the last two verses we are reminded that Amalek is to be totally destroyed. In Exodus 17 you will read that Amalek attacked the Israelites, and Israel had to fight back. At that time God said that the remembrance of Amalek was to be taken from under heaven, and this was the appointed time.

OFFERING THE FIRSTFRUITS
(Deuteronomy 26:1–11)

Why should a Christian thank God for every blessing?

Thanksgiving to God is proper at all times for everybody. We live in a country that has a national day of thanksgiving, and some people probably do not know that in this our country is unique. Deuteronomy 26 shows that thanksgiving to God is understood for people who live in His will. Thankfulness actually contributes to spiritual health. When the heart is not thankful to God the mind becomes vain and self-satisfied, and the person has spiritual troubles; but when the person practices giving glory to God he will not take it for himself. Do you know that when human beings come into the presence of God to be judged for the deeds done in the body, one of the things they are held responsible for is that they did not offer thanks?

In Deuteronomy 26:1–11 Moses instructed Israel on how to give thanks. They were to give thanks by presenting the firstfruits of their crops.

> That thou shalt take of the first of all the fruit of the earth, which thou shalt bring of thy land that the Lord thy God giveth thee, and shalt put it in a basket, and shalt go unto the place which the Lord thy God shall choose to place his name there (Deut. 26:2)

If a person has a garden and is raising beans, the first basket of beans he gets would be his firstfruits. In general, when one takes the firstfruits and gives them to anybody, it is a sort of special honor. Israel was trained to bring the firstfruits to God in thanksgiving.

> And the priest shall take the basket out of thine hand, and set it down before the altar of the Lord thy God. And thou shalt speak and say before the Lord thy God, A Syrian ready to perish was my father, and he went down into Egypt, and sojourned there with a few, and became there a nation, great, mighty, and populous (Deut. 26:4–5).

"A Syrian ready to perish was my father" refers to Jacob, who lived outside Palestine for a significant time. "And he went down into Egypt" refers to Jacob's sojourn when his son Joseph was in a high position there. The treatment accorded by the Egyptians was then recounted, as was how God heard the cry of the Hebrews and brought them out of Egypt with a mighty hand and gave them the land that flows with milk and honey. This was a sort of review of their personal experiences.

For us this means that when we come into the presence of God to thank Him we are to recall how God gave His Son to die for us. It is a good thing for us to stand in the presence of God and say, "I would have been lost, forever condemned from Thy presence, if it had not been that Thou didst send the

Lord Jesus Christ on my behalf, and I stand here thanking Thee because Christ Jesus died for me."

Having recounted the past, the Israelites were then to offer the firstfruits as a token of gratitude. They were to give the basket over to the priest.

> And now, behold, I have brought the firstfruits of the land, which thou, O Lord, hadst given me. And thou shalt set it before the Lord thy God, and worship before the Lord thy God: and thou shalt rejoice in every good thing which the Lord thy God hath given unto thee, and unto thine house, thou, and the Levite, and the stranger that is among you (Deut. 26:10–11).

And this is the will of God for us, also.

OFFERING THE TITHE
(Deuteronomy 26:12–15)

Do you think it is important to give to the Lord's work?

Giving to the Lord is an idea that is approved over and over again in the Bible. It is important to us because of the admonition we read in Scripture that we should heed it. Deuteronomy 26:12–15 brings up the matter of giving the tithe. Giving to the Lord is designed not so much to make God rich as it is to bring a blessing to the giver. When we give to the Lord we are implying that God is the giver of everything. God gives us everything, and if we put ten percent of our income into the Lord's work, this will glorify God.

Our giving to the Lord implies that we are fortunate. What we have, we have by the good grace of God. There are many people in the world as good as we are, who do not have what we have. We may not have as much as we want, and we may not have as much as we could use (though we probably have more than we deserve), but whatever we do have, we have from the Lord. And if we give to the Lord from our income, we are indicating that we think we are fortunate to have anything.

Furthermore, this matter of giving to the Lord develops a man's self-control. We are the boss of our money if we can give it away; if we cannot give it away, money is the boss of us. Furthermore, giving money to the Lord develops a man's obedience. When we do it because we think God wants us to do it, it will strengthen us. Another thing: if we give to the Lord today, we will qualify to receive more from Him tomorrow.

Now Moses instructed Israel to be thankful as they entered the land, and told them that being thankful would help them to be worthy of favor.

> When thou hast made an end of tithing all the tithes of thine increase the third year, which is the year of tithing, and hast given it unto the Levite, the stranger, the fatherless, and the widow, that they may eat within thy gates, and be filled; then thou shalt say before the Lord thy God, I have brought away the hallowed things out of mine house, and also have given them unto the Levite, and unto the stranger, to the fatherless, and to the widow, according to all thy commandments which thou hast commanded me: I have not transgressed thy commandments, neither have I forgotten them: I have not eaten thereof in my mourning, neither have I taken away aught thereof for any unclean use, nor given aught thereof for the dead: but I have hearkened to the voice of the Lord my God, and have done according to all that thou hast commanded me (Deut. 26:12–14).

A man can feel like that if he has honestly obeyed God.

> Look down from thy holy habitation, from heaven, and bless thy people Israel, and the land which thou hast given us, as thou swarest unto our fathers, a land that floweth with milk and honey (Deut. 26:15).

A person can pray to God for blessing after bringing this token of giving to Him. When we have learned to give, what we have left is enough; and we will not care about getting more, because we really are already being blessed.

COMMITTAL TO OBEDIENCE
(Deuteronomy 26:16–19)

Why is it so important for God's people to obey His will?
   When we are saved we become committed to do God's will.

The Bible shows that Almighty God the Creator made men in His own image, that men might do the will of God, even as His Son does the will of God.

I did not always understand God's plan. It seemed to me that God had made the world and put man in it, and then man did wrong, bringing about cause for his own destruction. God was anxious to save man from destruction, so He sent His own Son to die as a sacrifice so that man could be saved. I am not sure I had in mind even then what man would do when he was saved. I probably expected that man would be thankful about it and would want to please God. But I suspect I pretty much thought it was up to man as to what he would do.

When I look back on that now I realize I did not understand much about the gospel. I thought that when God made man He somehow turned him loose and expected man to do right on his own. Later He gave man the Ten Commandments telling man what to do and how to do. Then when man failed God sent His Son to save man from destruction. And from there I thought man was on his own to do the best he could. Many people think this way. They seem to have in mind that they are supposed to make the most they can of themselves. I am sure there are some who have an idea that somebody else is put in this world to paint a picture, or to serve for a length of time as president, or to do some great service for humankind. Men seem to feel that serving God is done strictly in their human efforts. Is that the way you feel?

Now consider that when God made this world, and when He made man and arranged to have him living in this world, it was God's intention that man would do the will of God. There seems to be no reason to doubt that. When man did fail and God sent His own Son into the world to save man and to show us what God is like, one characteristic about the Lord Jesus Christ was that He obeyed His Father. "I do always those things that please him" (John 8:29). Man, in his own vanity, sinned and sought to serve himself, and as a consequence, judgment was passed on all men. But God made a way out of this judgment.

> For God so loved the world, that he gave his only begotten Son, that whosoever believeth in him should not perish, but have everlasting life (John 3:16).

In Hebrews we read that the Son of God did not take on Him the nature of angels; He took on Him the nature of Abraham that He might taste death by dying for us. And thus we have the incarnation of God in the person of Jesus of Nazareth, and the death of Him as God and man. And Christ was resurrected from the dead by the power of God and ascended into the presence of God, where He is now interceding on our behalf. This is the course of God's program.

Because of this the sinner can come to the Lord Jesus Christ and actually belong to God.

> If any man will come after me, let him deny himself, and take up his cross, and follow me (Matt. 16:24).

The pattern is that the believer denies himself as he accepts Christ Jesus as Savior and Lord. He yields himself to Christ, actually crucifying his flesh with its affections and lust. Thus he is regenerated. To this regenerated person God gives the Holy Spirit, who comes to show him the things of Christ. The result then is that Christ is in him, the hope of glory. When this is the truth he can say,

> Beloved, now are we the sons of God, and it doth not yet appear what we shall be: but we know that, when he shall appear, we shall be like him; for we shall see him as he is (1 John 3:2).

Now man is yielded to God and committed to obey His will, so that as the apostle Paul could say:

> For as many as are led by the Spirit of God, they are the sons of God (Rom. 8:14).

And the Spirit of God leads the believer to obey God.

All that we find in the Christian gospel was explained by Moses to Israel when they entered the land of promise. Just as surely as they would keep the commandments, God would bless them. The first section of the Book of Deuteronomy showed that God had revealed His will in His Word. We should be careful how we receive His Word today, and we should follow it as our guide to daily living.

Here Moses speaks to the children of Israel just before they go into the land of promise.

> This day the Lord thy God hath commanded thee to do these

statutes and judgments: thou shalt therefore keep and do them with all thine heart, and with all thy soul. Thou hast avouched the Lord this day to be thy God, and to walk in his ways, and to keep his statutes, and his commandments, and his judgments, and to hearken unto his voice: and the Lord hath avouched thee this day to be his peculiar people, as he hath promised thee, and that thou shouldest keep all his commandments; and to make thee high above all nations which he hath made, in praise, and in name, and in honour; and that thou mayest be an holy people unto the Lord thy God, as he hath spoken (Deut. 26:16–19).

Because God gives us this promise today, we can say with the apostle John:

Behold, what manner of love the Father hath bestowed upon us, that we should be called the sons of God: therefore the world knoweth us not, because it knew him not (1 John 3:1).

Let us understand that we are committed to obey our Lord and Savior, Jesus Christ, and Almighty God our Father, and it will follow that we shall have peace and joy and blessing and communion with God.

CHAPTERS 27 and 28

† † †

MAKE A MONUMENT OF THE LAW
(Deuteronomy 27:1–8)

Have you ever thought about the significance of signs?

Some works of God, such as the processes of nature, are entirely within His own will and operation. The sun shines and the stars are in their places, and He does not ask man anything about that; those things go on whether men are awake or asleep. No personal response is needed. But salvation as a work of God must be received by man's response of putting faith in the Lord Jesus Christ.

Salvation is a matter of hearing, accepting, and believing the Word of God. A person is thus saved by the grace of God according to the promises that are in Christ Jesus, which are continuous. When you speak of a person being saved you may refer to the moment when that person put his trust in the Lord Jesus Christ. But from that time something is constantly going on in him, now and on into eternity: God is working in him to will and to do His good pleasure. It is this which makes him a believer.

We *come* to the Lord by hearing the Word and believing it, and so we *walk* in the Lord by remembering the Word and doing it. Living a consecrated life demands constant memory on the part of the person who is being brought near to God. This was illustrated by Moses when he talked to the children of Israel just before they entered the Promised Land. They were going to enter more into the will of God than their fathers ever had done.

Let us seriously consider the idea that it is possible to live closer to God tomorrow than you ever lived with Him before; you can actually grow in grace and knowledge. It may even be true for you that you are living in the desert day by day, trusting in God and every morning getting some manna from Him. You are being led by the cloud in the daytime and by the fire at night and are conscious of the help of God, yet you never feel very sure or secure, because you have not entered into the land that is flowing with milk and honey. Perhaps some day you will fully obey God and fully commit yourself to Him, and by Bible reading and prayer and seeking His face, you will truly walk with Him. This is the sort of experience the Book of Deuteronomy will help you toward. But if you are going to live that way tomorrow, you must know God's Word more fully and walk in faith more definitely than you did yesterday.

Moses knew that would be true with these people, and he was preparing them. When they crossed that river Jordan and went into the land they must from then on be always aware of God and His Word. The land was occupied by enemies, and the children of Israel would live in the presence of these enemies, needing help all the time. But God is invisible, and the promises of God are not yet, so a person who is going to walk with God must put his faith and trust in Someone he has not seen, expecting something that has not yet come to pass. And this is just what faith is, "the substance of things hoped for, the evidence of things not seen" (Heb. 11:1).

In Deuteronomy 27:1–8 are instructions these people were to follow that would enable them to remember the things of God.

> And Moses with the elders of Israel commanded the people, saying, Keep all the commandments which I command you this day (Deut. 27:1).

As a matter of fact this was saying to the people that they should consciously commit themselves, as far as they knew, to full obedience to the revealed will of God. A believer may not have in mind how he would recognize the will of God, but would he do His will if He showed it to him? Would he obey God? If so, he would see it would come to him.

On the day they entered the land they were to set up great stones, and plaster them as a memorial.

> And thou shalt write upon them all the words of this law . . . (Deut. 27:3).

Thus they were to make a great monument on which they were to spell out the words plainly, so that what God had said could be seen.

> And there shalt thou build an altar unto the Lord thy God, an altar of stones: thou shalt not lift up any iron tool upon them. Thou shalt build the altar of the Lord thy God of whole stones: and thou shalt offer burnt offerings thereon unto the Lord thy God (Deut. 27:5–6).

On this big monument of stone they were to carve the law of God, and right beside it they were to build an altar to worship. Can you see why? They would need the help of God to obey that law, and they would need the grace and mercy of God when they broke that law. This is good for us to keep in mind. No human being has the grace or the strength to do the will of God in himself; but anybody can do it with the help of God. So when you read the Word of God you must always read it prayerfully that you may understand it and receive it.

Moses commanded the Israelites not to use any iron tool in the construction of the altar. For man to have worked at the stones would have destroyed their God-created wholeness. We should not fix things up so much that we worship in some way we design, but we should open our hearts humbly and receive the truth of God as it is revealed. The people were to offer burnt offerings, which is the total commitment of the whole being. And they were to yield themselves fully to God and offer peace offerings and eat and rejoice.

Consecrated living involves continuous obedience to the living will of the living God.

DRAMATIZE THE ISSUE CLEARLY
(Deuteronomy 27:9–26)

Can you see that sometimes a sign that says "Stop" would be the best kind of guidance for you?

Walking with the Lord is liberty. People who walk with the Lord rejoice in the liberty wherein Christ has made them free, but I wonder whether they realize that they are free because they have turned away from their own ideas. Liberty in Christ Jesus is only for the spiritual person. A person who still has his human nature does not have that liberty, because his human nature goes one way and the Spirit of the Lord goes the other. Such a person has in him continuous strain and stress. And this is the case with many people. They still have their human nature which wants to do what pleases them, yet they also have some knowledge of the Word of God and want to do what pleases the Lord. Thus they are torn between these two desires.

A believer who really wants to walk with the Lord will have to first of all give his human nature a sharp, implacable *no*! Then, when he has turned away from his sinful nature, he has the privilege of "whatsoever thy hand finds to do, do it with all thy might."

You may well wonder again why the Ten Commandments given on Mount Sinai were put in negative form like so many stop signs. Living in Christ is traveling along the road of the will of God. We have curbs to keep us from going off the street and stop signs to keep us from going into the wrong place at the wrong time.

The gospel includes both "Don't go here" and "Go into all the world." With reference to the natural, the Bible says "don't," and with reference to the spiritual the Bible says "go." Again it is just like traveling: the traveler sees the sign that says "Danger," which is telling him not to go off into the ditch; then he sees in another place, a sign that says the city is twenty-five miles down the road. He can go as far as he wants on that highway until he reaches the city.

Moses, in trying to help the people understand the ways of God, reminded them that when they begin to obey they already belong to God:

> . . . O Israel; this day thou art become the people of the Lord thy God (Deut. 27:9).

This is like what happens in the wedding ceremony when the bride says "I do." She becomes the wife of the husband without further word.

Moses used various methods to impress upon Israel that it would be up to them to walk more in the will of God than others had done in the past. He told them plainly that when they walked into that land they would belong to God and would be called the people of God. At Moses' command six of the tribes gathered on top of Mount Gerizim and six gathered on top of Mount Ebal. All Israel was on one side of the valley or the other: this was a way of bringing to their mind there was no middle ground for them. Then one of the priests led them through an exercise in which he pronounced a curse, and all the people on Mount Ebal said "Amen"; then the contrary blessing was pronounced and the people on Mount Gerizim said "Amen." In this dramatic yet simple way Moses set before the children of Israel that either they would do the will of God and be blessed, or they would not do the will of God and be cursed. There are twelve successive statements in verses 15 to 26 regarding the consequences of doing wrong. There may have been more than twelve; those listed are at least examples.

The negative aspect of guidance—"Thou shalt not"—can keep a person out of all kinds of trouble. "Stop" leaves a person much more liberty than "Go." When a person comes to a place where a sign says "Do not enter," what choices does that leave him? He can go anywhere else in the world, just not there. But if the sign says "Go this way," he cannot go any other place and expect blessing. The positive command to go is much more binding than the negative command which says don't go. In spite of all other theories about guidance, there is still one elemental truth: obeying "Thou shalt not" leaves a person with the greater liberty, because he can then do anything else that is good that he wants to do.

BLESSING UPON OBEDIENCE
(Deuteronomy 28:1–14)

Do you realize how wonderful is the blessing of God?

> The blessing of the Lord, it maketh rich, and he addeth no sorrow with it (Prov. 10:22).

By staying on the right road you can have the whole world

before you. The decision to walk with the Lord is something a person makes consciously, while daily fellowship with God is oftentimes almost unconscious. This constant fellowship that you have with God, walking in His presence, is a case of trusting and depending on Him and having unending good fortune as a result.

Entering into the land was a dramatic occasion for the children of Israel, and living there in the will of God was something that would go on and on, yet never become monotonous. It could be a continuous triumph of blessing. Believers, too, can say that the blessings of the Lord are fresh every morning like dew on the grass. Have you experienced that in your own life? Do you have such a personal fellowship with the Lord? When the day comes to a close are you able to feel in your heart that God has been with you, so that you can say over and over according to the word, we remember as Ebenezer, "Hitherto hath the Lord helped us"? (I Sam. 7:12).

Moses prepared the children of Israel to enter the land of promise walking with God. He wanted them to come with full appreciation of what they were doing, and to celebrate it in an important way.

> And it shall come to pass, if thou shalt hearken diligently unto the voice of the Lord thy God, to observe and to do all his commandments which I command thee this day, that the Lord thy God will set thee on high above all nations of the earth: and all these blessings shall come on thee, and overtake thee, if thou shalt hearken unto the voice of the Lord thy God (Deut. 28:1-2).

Moses then listed the blessings that were to come upon them. They would be set high above all others if they would keep all God's commandments. What that boils down to in our day is willingness to obey God. When the believer turns his heart over to God in the Lord Jesus Christ, God puts into him the Holy Spirit who will incline his heart in the way of God.

So again, the prerequisite for believers to receive the blessing of God is a willingness to obey Him. What they can look forward to is that "the Lord will set thee on high above all" if they do just this one thing: hearken unto the voice of God. A believer can do this in his home or in his office; he does not even have to have his Bible in his hand. He can accept the very circumstances under which he is living as being the situation that God has prepared for him and accept his daily task as something God has given him to do.

Deuteronomy 28:7–9 sets forth a list of the blessings Israel was to receive. Enemies were to be smitten as indicated by this expression: ". . . they shall come out against thee one way, and flee before thee seven ways" (Deut. 28:7). In other words, enemies would be scattered and Israel would have the protection of God. Verse 8 says that they were to be blessed in their storehouses; they would have plenty of what they needed. Today's believers can still count on this promise: if they walk with the Lord He will watch over them. They may not have as much as they want, and they may not have as much as their neighbors, but they will have plenty of what they need.

Deuteronomy 28:9–10 promises Israel will be established as a holy people unto the Lord, separated to Him, and called by His name over all the earth. Today when anybody calls a person a Christian, he uses the name of Christ in the very word, linking this person with Him.

In the Old Testament most of the blessings were temporal. The ways in which Israel could see that they were being blessed were when they had good crops and the trees had an abundance of fruit and when the cattle had many calves and the sheep had many lambs. Living in New Testament times under the new covenant you and I may find our major blessings are spiritual, although this does not rule out the temporal. Believers in Christ may have temporal blessings also, but they will have complete fulfillment if they have peace and joy and blessedness in their hearts.

> . . . thou shalt be above only, and thou shalt not be beneath; if that thou hearken unto the commandments of the Lord thy God . . . and not go aside . . . to go after other gods (Deut. 28:13–14).

No man can have God's blessings if his heart wanders away from God.

CURSES UPON DISOBEDIENCE
(Deuteronomy 28:15–68)

Do you think there is such a thing as the curse of God?

The Bible tells us the wrath of God comes on all children of disobedience. My heart is impressed that there is no one truth about God that is so much neglected and misrepresented today as this one. On almost every side there is sentiment that the curse of God is out of date. But we know that the Bible reveals to us the Word of God, and it is in the Bible that we learn about the wrath of God. He dealt with Adam and Eve and with the serpent in the Garden of Eden. We remember the great day of judgment when God sent the flood. He destroyed Sodom and Gomorrah. He destroyed the Canaanites and afterwards destroyed Israel and sent Judah into captivity. Some dismiss this line of truth as Old Testament teaching, but it is also in the New Testament.

On one occasion the Lord Jesus Christ made it plain there would be certain conditions under which,

> . . . it were better for him that a millstone were hanged about his neck, and that he were drowned in the depth of the sea (Matt. 18:6).

Make no mistake about it, the wrath of God comes upon the children of disobedience. In Deuteronomy Moses tried to make the people realize that while God blessed people, it was also true that He would bring distress upon people.

We speak of the curse from God as we speak of the promises of God, and in a certain sense the curse is a promise. We usually use the word *promise* for that which is good, but actually what we have in a promise is that God has let it be known beforehand what He will do. He has let it be known beforehand that He will bless certain things and He will not bless other things. And so for the one we use the word *blessing*, and for the other we use the word *curse*.

"Whatsoever a man soweth, that shall he also reap" (Gal. 6:7). If a man sows of the flesh, he shall of the flesh reap corruption (wrath); and if a man sows of the Spirit, he shall of the Spirit reap life everlasting (blessing). Both are under the justice and righteousness of God. We are to understand that God will add to evil more evil, just as He adds to good more good. When we plant a garden we get a crop because God blesses it. A believer will not have any hesitancy in saying that God produces that crop. But if we have thistles in the garden and their seeds fall into the ground, we have more thistles. Where do additional thistles come from? Is it not true that the new thistles came from the processes of God just as more beans came from the processes of God? If beans will produce more beans, thistles will also produce more thistles. The same God who causes the food to grow in your garden is the same God who allows the weeds to grow in your garden.

The Bible says that God has no pleasure in people going to hell, but there will be those who will be destroyed because it is just. It is wonderful to know that whosoever believes in the Lord Jesus Christ will be saved. We can remember that the grace of the Lord Jesus Christ is greater than all our sins and that though our "sins be as scarlet, they shall be as white as snow; though they be red like crimson, they shall be as wool" (Isa. 1:18). We thank the Lord we can be saved from the wrath of God, but the wrath of God is real. We see this in the book of Romans, where we read that in the gospel "the wrath of God is revealed from heaven against all ungodliness and un-righteousness of men" (Rom. 1:18).

In Romans 5 we read that one of the wonderful things about the Lord Jesus Christ is that living as He does now in the presence of God He is able to save from wrath (the conse-quences of evil deeds) those who put their trust in Him. One of the earliest statements in the Bible is "the soul that sinneth, it shall die" (Ezek. 18:4). The last verses in chapter 28 are sad reading:

> But it shall come to pass, if thou wilt not hearken unto the voice of the Lord thy God, to observe to do all his command-ments and his statutes which I command thee this day; that all these curses shall come upon thee, and overtake thee (Deut. 28:15).

The curse of God will come upon disobedience, but the hum-ble and contrite heart God will not despise.

> And thou shalt become an astonishment, a proverb, and a byword, among all nations whither the Lord shall lead thee (Deut. 28:37).

Then follows verse after verse telling the terrible results of disobedience. The lesson for us is that if we are not obedient to the Lord our God, we, too, will suffer greatly.

> Thou shalt carry much seed out into the field, and shalt gather but little in . . . Thou shalt plant vineyards, and dress them, but shalt neither drink of the wine, nor gather the grapes; for the worms shall eat them (Deut. 28:38-39).

This passage shows that just as an obedient Israel would be an example of blessing, a disobedient Israel would be an example of distress. In Deuteronomy 28:47–57 we learn that if Israel would not serve God with joy they would have to serve others in sorrow. Truly the way of the transgressor is hard.

CHAPTERS 29 and 30

† † †

THE COVENANT FOR BLESSING
(Deuteronomy 29:1–9)

Do you realize there are certain conditions under which the blessing of God is received?

The blessing of God is available to all, but do all receive it? The blessing of God comes to all who respond to His guidance, to those who obey Him. God made the whole universe and all natural processes. A man who is ungodly will work a grain field and by doing the right things naturally, he can reap a good crop. God gave him that crop, but it was not related to any personal faithfulness on the man's part. He was faithful to God only with respect to the laws of nature. "Whatsoever a man soweth, that shall he also reap," and any man who expects to prosper must work.

But there is one thing man can't work for—salvation. Salvation is a free gift of the grace of God in Christ Jesus. It is offered in promise and received in faith. In the New Testament Paul argues definitely that if you had to work for salvation, it would not be by grace; but if you receive it by faith, it is the grace of God.

On the night of the Passover, when the firstborn throughout all the land were to die, Moses gave instructions to the Israelites to put the blood of the Passover lamb on their doorposts and over the top of their doors so that the firstborn would be spared when the angel of death passed through the land. No special attention would be paid to the character of the persons inside marked houses; the angel of death would see the blood and would pass over them. In the same way redemption is a free gift of God to those who respond by believing in the blood of the Lord Jesus Christ.

God did not give Moses the Ten Commandments on Mount Sinai with the intent that anyone of that time who would keep them would be acceptable in the sight of God. Rather the law was given to people already accepted by God. He had delivered them out of the land of Egypt and they were walking in faith. Every night the pillar of fire had led them, and every day the cloud had been over them. Because they were like children, and there would be many things they would not know about pleasing God, He gave them the Ten Words to guide them in their conduct and promised them He would bless them as long as they were obedient to those Ten Words.

At Mount Sinai they had learned that communion with God is a gift; and now, in the land of Moab just before entering into the land of Canaan, Moses gave them another promise: they would receive prosperity as a gift when they responded to the call of God.

We should bear in mind that what Moses was teaching was that blessing would come from God in response to their faith. In Deuteronomy 29 these things are spelled out plainly. In the first verse we read that this covenant would be made in the land of Moab beside the one made at Horeb. They were then reminded that they had seen all that the Lord had done for them since their time of slavery in Egypt. The history of the exodus would strengthen them to believe God and to trust in Him. Yet they apparently did not yet have the capacity to understand this, and for this reason they were given even more specific instructions. Moses then cautioned the people:

> Keep therefore the words of this covenant, and do them, that
> ye may prosper in all that ye do (Deut. 29:9).

Obedient response to the revealed will of God brings blessing. We must keep in mind that walking with the Lord brings constant guidance by His Holy Spirit, and as we follow the guidance of the Holy Spirit we can expect His continuous blessing.

PROMISE OF JUDGMENT
UPON DISOBEDIENCE
(Deuteronomy 29:10–28)

Granted we believe the promises of God, do you think we should heed the warnings also?

Growing in faith brings responsibility for each of us. After a believer belongs to Him and God gives him the Holy Spirit, God expects that believer to bear fruit. Deuteronomy 29:10–13 sets forth that walking with the Lord will demand 100 percent of the believer's attention. Moses gave a complete list of the people who were to respond to the will of God.

> Ye stand this day all of you before the Lord your God; your captains of your tribes, your elders, and your officers, with all the men of Israel, your little ones, your wives, and thy stranger that is in thy camp, from the hewer of thy wood unto the drawer of thy water (Deut. 29:10–11).

Even their friends were to be chosen from among the people who wanted to obey God. They did not need to claim that they were perfect; that was not the point. Moses was talking about total commitment.

In Deuteronomy 29:14–20 we read that anyone turning back would be dealt God's judgment. Once the Israelites started walking with the Lord it was expected that they would continue walking with Him.

> Lest there should be among you man, or woman, or family, or tribe, whose heart turneth away this day from the Lord our God, to go and serve the gods of these nations; lest there should be among you a root that beareth gall and wormwood (Deut. 29:18).

Moses pointed out that a person could actually turn away from God even if he did not do it openly; he could forsake God in his heart.

> And it come to pass, when he heareth the words of this curse, that he bless himself in his heart, saying, I shall have peace, though I walk in the imagination of mine heart, to add drunkenness to thirst (Deut. 29:19).

Some people, even when they hear the Word preached, may conform outwardly just to please men. But God sees their hearts and their mental reservations, and He will judge them accordingly.

> The Lord will not spare him, but then the anger of the Lord and his jealousy shall smoke against that man, and all the curses that are written in this book shall lie upon him, and the Lord shall blot out his name from under heaven (Deut. 29:20).

Moses continued to give definite warning from God that He would make an example of such defectors that all men could see. Men would know that the cursed ones once belonged to God but had not been faithful.

Serving other gods will bring judgment from God in the form of sickness upon the land. I am not sure how we should understand that in our day, and I am not sure we can tell who is being blessed and who is not being blessed, but I am satisfied that God knows. Certainly it is true that if men disobey and turn away from God, He will judge them.

This is an ominous omission in the modern message. Many times when people offer new ideas about the gospel or about Christian living, I wait to hear if they will say that when a man turns away from God, God will judge him. That is the truth, and we need to keep it in mind. Those who want to walk with God must be on guard lest they fall into some snare like this. After a person has joined the church and has started walking with the Lord, he may begin to alibi for himself. He does not do the things God wants him to do, but he says he has good reasons for not doing them. He explains this to himself, while keeping up the outward appearances of doing right. But God looks on the heart of every believer and He will judge those who turn away from Him.

REVELATION HELPS OBEDIENCE
(Deuteronomy 29:29)

Do you think that anyone will ever find out everything?
I now draw your attention to the last verse of chapter 29:

> The secret things belong unto the Lord our God: but those

> things which are revealed belong unto us and to our children
> for ever, that we may do all the words of this law (Deut. 29:29).

We live in a day of many discoveries; some of which are good,
while others are evil. Men have found answers for some of
life's most perplexing questions, yet much remains secret.
Take, for instance, the spontaneous free choices of people.
With all the insight in the world one does not know what any
person will do in a given circumstance. Inside the human
heart is the will to do as one wants to do.

There are other things we are not able to find out about,
among them, the origin of the universe. Regardless of how
much discussion we hear, we still wonder about that. And
the destiny of the universe: who knows? Then there is God
Himself, who remains invisible not only to our eyes but in
other ways. And even man himself is difficult to understand. So we will say there are some things we will never
know.

Natural processes apparently can be known by man and
can be manipulated as is done in science. But there are
things about God that we would never know if He had not
revealed it. In Christ Jesus God has revealed His plan to
save. And Christ Jesus has been revealed in the Scriptures.
But much more has been revealed about God in Scripture.
For instance, we can learn about His nature—that He loves
and cares for us and wants to redeem and have fellowship
with us. Scripture also reveals how the Son of God took on
Him the form of man that He might be able in Himself to
accomplish the deliverance of man. We learn that Christ
lived in that human nature perfectly according to what the
law of God required.

"The secret things belong unto the Lord our God. [Much
about our life we will never know, and we do not need to
know.] But those things which are revealed [His plan to
save us in Christ Jesus] belong unto us and to our children
for ever, that we may do all the words of this law." You and
I can actually fulfill the law of God by trusting in the Lord
Jesus Christ; and this is how it happens: we believe in the
Lord Jesus Christ, He keeps the law perfectly, and He allows
us to share in the perfect righteousness that He has before
God.

PROMISE OF GRACE UPON OBEDIENCE
(Deuteronomy 30:1–10)

Do you realize that anybody can turn to God and be saved?

The gospel of the Lord Jesus Christ is for the whole world. We have no hesitation in saying, "whosoever will may come." We realize that when many hear this they think in terms of being saved from final destruction, and many will turn to God without fully realizing what it means. Christ died not only to save us from destruction, but to bring us into fellowship with Him.

The prospect of being saved from destruction is a powerful thing. But the promise is "whosoever believeth in Him shall not perish but have everlasting life" (John 3:16). Some persons, when the fear of hell is gone, seem to feel that all is done, but this is not the end of salvation.

Let us consider Israel. When they reached Kadesh-Barnea, two years after leaving Egypt, they did not have the faith to go forward into the land of Canaan. Most of us know persons who have accepted Christ as their Savior, and then later they seem to lapse into unbelief. The unbelief is about living in the Lord. They started out walking with Him, but now no longer do so. Other ideas have come into their minds; some have turned to other gods. Moses realized that the children of Israel, after coming into the land of Canaan, might take up the habits of the pagans there. Likewise, there are those today who, in trouble, turn to the Lord and become believers; but after the trial is over they become worldly. Moses warned Israel that God would cast such out.

Chapter 30 contains a wonderful message.

> And it shall come to pass, when all these things are come upon thee, the blessing and the curse, which I have set before thee, and thou shalt call them to mind among all the nations, whither the Lord thy God hath driven thee, and shalt return unto the Lord thy God, and shalt obey his voice according to all that I command thee this day, thou and thy children, with all thine heart, and with all thy soul; that then the Lord thy God will turn thy captivity, and have compassion upon thee, and will return and gather thee from all the nations, whither the Lord thy God hath scattered thee (Deut. 30:1–3).

Here is the promise that God would take them back to Himself:

> If any of thine be driven out unto the outmost parts of heaven, from thence will the Lord thy God gather thee, and from thence will he fetch thee: and the Lord thy God will bring thee into the land which thy fathers possessed, and thou shalt possess it; and he will do thee good, and multiply thee above thy fathers (Deut. 30:4–5).

What we are reading here is a promise that revival is possible. The erring believer can actually be restored to God. The prodigal son can come home, and his father will receive him. Moses knew he would not be with Israel all the time, so he brought all this out that they would know that if they disobeyed God, He would deal chastisement; but if then they turned back to God, He would receive and change them.

> And the Lord thy God will circumcise thine heart, and the heart of thy seed, to love the Lord thy God with all thine heart, and with all thy soul, that thou mayest live (Deut. 30:6).

> And thou shalt return and obey the voice of the Lord, and do all his commandments which I command thee this day. And the Lord thy God will make thee plenteous in every work of thine hand, in the fruit of thy body, and in the fruit of thy cattle, and in the fruit of thy land, for good: for the Lord will again rejoice over thee for good, as he rejoiced over thy fathers: if thou shalt hearken unto the voice of the Lord thy God, to keep his commandments and his statutes which are written in this book of the law, and if thou turn unto the Lord thy God with all thine heart, and with all thy soul (Deut. 30:8–10).

If any believer once lived closer to God than he does now, he can come back. God knows where he is, and is willing to show Himself strong on behalf of those who put their trust in Him.

PLAIN TALK ABOUT THE GOSPEL
(Deuteronomy 30:11–20)

Do you know how simple the gospel really is?

When I was an unbeliever I had the impression that the things of religion were obscure, and any talk about the Bible would be something I would not understand. And I thought nobody else understood much about it either. It seemed that whenever I heard religious arguments of one sort or another, there was no end to the discussion, no agreement was reached.

Actually, salvation is simple. While I was at work recently a phone call came from a young woman who described herself as a business woman. She had suddenly become tired; everything seemed futile and empty. Her mother had persuaded her to return from New York and come to talk to me. Her problem was that she could not believe in God. When I asked if she ever read about these things she gave me the names of popular authors, all of whom were notorious for not believing the Bible. It bothered her that such intelligent men could not believe, and because of that she too found it hard to believe.

I then asked her if she realized that she could be within two blocks of the Empire State Building in New York on a bright day and still not see it. She thought a moment then said, "Do you mean if I had my back turned to it?" I replied, "Exactly. If you had your back turned to it you could take a telescope and still not see it. It would be a matter of which way you were looking. Now why don't you look at Jesus Christ?" She got the point right away and wanted to know where to find out about Him. I suggested that she read the four Gospels for a start. Now I want to pass this on to you: If you will look at the Lord Jesus Christ and put your trust in Him, you will have everything needful for salvation.

Moses tried to make it plain to his people. In chapter 30 we read,

> For this commandment which I command thee this day, it is not hidden from thee, neither is it far off (Deut. 30:11).

There is nothing secretive about the Christian gospel.

> But the word is very nigh unto thee, in thy mouth, and in thy heart, that thou mayest do it. See, I have set before thee this day life and good, and death and evil (Deut. 30:14–15).

All along Moses had been telling the Israelites to obey the voice of God and they would be blessed; disobey the voice of God and they would be cursed. There is a narrow road that leads to life and a wide road that leads to destruction. Which are you on?

> In that I command thee this day to love the Lord thy God, to walk in his ways, and to keep his commandments and his statutes and his judgments, that thou mayest live and multiply: and the Lord thy God shall bless thee in the land whither thou goest to possess it (Deut. 30:16).

That is the promise: walk with God and be blessed.

> But if thine heart turn away, so that thou wilt not hear, but shalt be drawn away, and worship other gods, and serve them; I denounce unto you this day, that ye shall surely perish, and that ye shall not prolong your days upon the land, whither thou passest over Jordan to go to possess it. I call heaven and earth to record this day against you, that I have set before you life and death, blessing and cursing: therefore choose life, that both thou and thy seed may live (Deut. 30:17–19).

You may know persons who have become disobedient and have turned away. You should turn your heart to God and let your light shine before them. Bring them before the Lord God in prayer every day and trust in the Lord Jesus Christ. You do not know everything and you cannot do everything, but God does know the needs of every believer and can and will meet them. There is before you today a blessing and a curse—life and death. If you turn to God, He will turn to you. If you draw nigh unto God, He will draw nigh unto you. Put your trust in the Lord Jesus Christ, and He will save your soul.

CHAPTERS 31 and 32

† † †

GOD WILL GO WITH YOU
(Deuteronomy 31:1–8)

Why may Christians look forward to tomorrow with confidence?

Changes can occur suddenly, and no man knows what a day will bring forth. Because of this, some have no peace in their hearts, as there is dread about the future in its place. Why do consecrated believers have peace about tomorrow? Is it because they know what will happen and are ready for it, or is it because they know who will be there when it happens? Some of us, not satisfied with what has happened until now, wish that we might be able to live nearer to God tomorrow than we did yesterday. And that is possible. But it can only be accomplished if we will act differently than we acted yesterday.

Let us notice closely what Moses has to say to Israel. Moses told the people they would have to accept different leadership in the future. And we should note for ourselves, that if we want to turn our heart over to the Lord and live in Him with all sincerity, we will have to expect to be led in a different way. We will need to act according to the Holy Spirit within us. We may not always know what it is He wants us to do, but we will hear, as it were, a voice within saying, "This is the way, walk ye in it."

Moses prepared his people for the change in leadership.

> And he said unto them, I am a hundred and twenty years old this day; I can no more go out and come in: also the Lord hath said unto me "Thou shalt not go over this Jordan. The Lord thy God, he will go over before thee, and he will destroy these nations from before thee, and thou shalt possess them: and Joshua, he shall go over before thee, as the Lord hath said (Deut. 31:2-3).

Their enemies would be destroyed.

> And the Lord shall give them up before your face, that ye may
> do unto them according unto all the commandments which I
> have commanded you (Deut. 31:5).

We are to move forward in fellowship with the Lord. Of
course reading our Bible is part of drawing closer, but we are
also to listen to the voice of God within our soul. For the
Israelites, Joshua was different from Moses; for us, the Holy
Spirit will lead into further growth after we have accepted the
Lord Jesus Christ.

> Be strong and of a good courage, fear not, nor be afraid of them:
> for the Lord thy God, he it is that doth go with thee; he will not
> fail thee, nor forsake thee (Deut. 31:6).

Wonderful promises! Moses then had something to say to
Joshua:

> Be strong and of a good courage: for thou must go with this
> people unto the land which the Lord hath sworn unto their
> fathers to give them; and thou shalt cause them to inherit it.
> And the Lord, he it is that doth go before thee; he will be with
> thee, he will not fail thee, neither forsake thee: fear not,
> neither be dismayed (Deut. 31:7–8).

Believers are blessed with this confidence not because they
know more than other people or because they are better or
stronger, but because they trust in the Lord and understand
that the Lord will go with them.

PROGRAM OF EDUCATION
(Deuteronomy 31:9–15)

Do you realize the importance of reading the Bible?

Spiritual living is a matter of faith, of believing God. "Without faith it is impossible to please Him." Believing has the
same relation to your spiritual life that swallowing does to
your physical life. If someone were to ask how you live, you
could say in one sense that you live by swallowing, but that is
not the whole story. You must swallow pure food; poisonous

food would make you sick and possibly cause death. Believing is very much like that. We are saved by believing, but it is not believing just anything; it is believing the gospel. Believing a lie will result in loss, while believing in the Lord Jesus Christ will save your soul. How can a person believe? According to Paul, only if one has heard the gospel. And the gospel is found nowhere but in the Bible. In the Bible we read:

> Eye hath not seen, nor ear heard, neither have entered into the heart of man, the things which God hath prepared for them that love him. But God hath revealed them unto us by his Spirit: for the Spirit searcheth all things, yea, the deep things of God (1 Cor. 2:9-10).

In order to believe in God a person must know what God has said. The more a person understands what is in the Bible, the more he understands what has been revealed about God. In the course of these studies in Deuteronomy Moses has been instructing Israel how to live when they enter into the land, where they will live by faith. To live by faith they will have to know what God has said.

> And Moses wrote this law, and delivered it unto the priests the sons of Levi, which bare the ark of the covenant of the Lord, and unto all the elders of Israel (Deut. 31:9).

Moses instructed them how to read the law at the Feast of Tabernacles.

> When all Israel is come to appear before the Lord thy God in the place which he shall choose, thou shalt read this law before all Israel in their hearing. Gather the people together, men, and women, and children, and thy stranger that is within thy gates, that they may hear, and that they may learn, and fear the Lord your God, and observe to do all the words of this law (Deut. 31:11-12).

When you read the Bible reverently and try to understand it, you will hear the Word of God and learn His promises. Then you can be careful to perform the things that are written therein. The importance of reading the Bible then is that your own faith and understanding might grow, that you might become more and more committed to doing the will of God, that you might reverence the Lord God, and that your children who hear you read will listen and watch as you apply it. Children with no other training than what they get in the home can understand the Word and will respect and honor the Lord and serve Him.

PREPARATION FOR FUTURE APOSTASY
(Deuteronomy 31:16–30)

Do you realize there is no way to keep people from going astray?

At Kadesh-Barnea when the twelve spies went into Canaan to investigate, ten said, "We cannot enter the land," but two were faithful and said it could be done. Moses knew that when the people finally entered the land the day would come when they would wander away from God, and he prepared for that by giving them instructions. Deuteronomy 31:14-15 records that the time had come for Moses to die. He was told to call Joshua and to instruct him in taking over the leadership.

> And the Lord said unto Moses, Behold, thou shalt sleep with thy fathers; and this people will rise up . . . and will forsake me . . . and I will hide my face from them (Deut. 31:16–17).

In the New Testament the apostle Paul had a similar warning for some of the early church leaders.

> Take heed therefore unto yourselves, and to all the flock, over the which the Holy Ghost hath made you overseers, to feed the church of God, which he hath purchased with his own blood. For I know this, that after my departing shall grievous wolves enter in among you, not sparing the flock. Also of your own selves shall men arise, speaking perverse things, to draw away disciples after them (Acts 20:28–30).

God told Moses to write His revelation of apostasy in a song and teach it to the people. They should teach it to their children that it might be a witness unto them.

> Now therefore write ye this song for you, and teach it the children of Israel: put it in their mouths, that this song may be a witness for me against the children of Israel (Deut. 31:19).

When troubles later came to the children of Israel this song of Moses would tell them the truth.

Deuteronomy 31:23 gave encouragement to Joshua. In spite of the fact that the people would turn away from God Joshua was told:

> Be strong and of a good courage: for thou shalt bring the children of Israel into the land which I sware unto them: and I will be with thee (Deut. 31:23).

The people might be disposed to wander away from God, but Joshua would yet lead them through.

Deuteronomy 31:24–30 shows how Moses called all the elders and the officers to come together that he might speak certain words in their ears:

> For I know thy rebellion. . . . after my death ye will utterly corrupt yourselves . . . ye will do evil in the sight of the Lord, to provoke him to anger through the work of your hands (Deut. 31:27–29).

We may wonder why Moses told them such things. When there is prospect of people turning away from God, frank, realistic handling is the most constructive way to deal with that problem. When people are turning away from God is no time for flattery.

THE FOOLISH PERVERSITY OF GOD'S PEOPLE
(Deuteronomy 32:1–28)

Do you realize that it is when men become prosperous that they are inclined to be foolish?

We understand that it is by the power of God that a man is saved. As men believe in God and respond to the revealed will of God, they are blessed. But we need to keep in mind that such blessings do not necessarily change the human heart. When I pick up a ball rolling along the ground and then put it back down it will go on rolling downhill. The ball does not change because I hold it in my hand. The human being is something like that.

I know there is such a thing as being born again, and I certainly believe in the new life that is in Christ, but I am talking about the human nature of a person. When I am born again, the new man in me is from God, but the old man in me is like he always was. He has the same tendencies he always had. By the grace of God believers can overcome the old man, and by the Holy Spirit they can walk in the ways of God. But consecration to God is not necessarily a permanent condition. A yielded person can wander because the human nature of man is fickle, easily diverted.

If you and I are to walk with the Lord we will do so because we believe in Him and are committed to Him. All this is a matter of faith. The stronger our faith is, the better off we are; the weaker it is, the more danger we have. Our faithfulness needs constant nourishment. Faith is nourished by the Word of God. Any time we neglect attentive Bible reading our faith will get weaker, and we can falter. Then the old man in us will take over and we will sin. To realize that we are liable to fall helps us to avoid it.

Moses wrote the song the Lord told him to write to describe how the people would wander away from God, and how God would bring them back to Him. The people would be so foolish that, having begun with God, they could turn away. Years later they would remember the song and how they could return to God. In this song Moses exalted the name of the Lord, and ascribed greatness to Him.

> He is the Rock, his work is perfect: for all his ways are judgment: a God of truth and without iniquity, just and right is he (Deut. 32:4).

Moses gave praise to God for His righteousness, His holiness, His justice, and His truth. He also set forth a description of the people who would fail God.

> They have corrupted themselves, their spot is not the spot of his children: they are a perverse and crooked generation. Do ye thus requite the Lord, O foolish people and unwise? Is not he thy father that hath bought thee? hath he not made thee, and established thee? (Deut. 32:5-6).

There was no reason for these people to turn away from Him, but they did.

Moses then recalled what had happened in the past. This was something for the people to keep in mind even when they were doing wrong. They should remember what God did when first He called them.

Remember the days of old, consider the years of many generations: ask thy father, and he will show thee; thy elders, and
they will tell thee. When the Most High divided to the nations
their inheritance, when he separated the sons of Adam, he set
the bounds of the people according to the number of the children of Israel. For the Lord's portion is his people; Jacob is the
lot of his inheritance (Deut. 32:7–9).

Then Moses told how God had blessed Jacob.

He found him in a desert land, and in the waste howling wilderness; he led him about, he instructed him, he kept him as
the apple of his eye. As an eagle stirreth up her nest, fluttereth
over her young, spreadeth abroad her wings, taketh them,
beareth them on her wings: so the Lord alone did lead him,
and there was no strange god with him. He made him ride on
the high places of the earth, that he might eat the increase of
the fields; and he made him to suck honey out of the rock, and
oil out of the flinty rock; butter of kine, and milk of sheep, with
fat of lambs, and rams of the breed of Bashan, and goats, with
the fat of kidneys of wheat; and thou didst drink the pure blood
of the grape (Deut. 32:10–14).

This detailed menu showed how rich and satisfying their food
was when they were blessed of God. Then Moses included in
the song which they were to sing:

But Jeshurun waxed fat, and kicked: thou art waxen fat, thou
art grown thick, thou art covered with fatness; then he forsook
God which made him, and lightly esteemed the Rock of his
salvation (Deut. 32:15).

"Jeshurun" is another name for Jacob. When I read that Israel
had little regard for God I am reminded of today's society.
Many fellow-believers I know would never deliberately turn
against God, but they would leave the Bible in the church,
and lightly esteem it. Going to church would become a social
affair, and the preacher would talk about anything but God.
The reading of the Bible and prayers would be brief, so as not
to bother the people. This is lightly esteeming the Rock of our
salvation.

Deuteronomy 32:20–28 reveals that God will actually
judge the people. It is a sad story of what He will do. All of
this was put into a hymn, and they were to sing it, so that
in days to come they might be reminded of the truth of
God.

THE GRACIOUS MERCY OF GOD
(Deuteronomy 32:29–43)

Have you ever noticed that sudden calamity will turn some people away from foolishness?

At this point in our study of Deuteronomy Moses is warning the children of Israel that they would foolishly turn away from God and that God would need to deal with them inasmuch as He promised He would keep them. In a song, or poem, Moses recorded God's revelation of Israel's apostasy so that years later they would have it in their memories. In the New Testament we read, "For whom the Lord loveth he chasteneth, and scourgeth every son whom he receiveth" (Heb. 12:6). When a person after knowing God turns away to foolishness, he should really be destroyed for he had his opportunity but turned away. But God, in mercy, sends calamity upon that foolish, wayward person to cause him to repent and turn back to God.

We remember the story of how the prodigal son came to his senses in the very depths of distress. Oftentimes a believer will not be stopped in his foolishness until calamity occurs. We are glad that the administration of such affairs is in the hands of God. Do you know that your prayers may result in God bringing calamity upon a loved one? God in mercy sometimes has to send calamity to awaken people out of their foolishness. These things were implied in the song Moses gave to the people before they went into the land.

Let us consider again how strange this is. The whole purpose of Israel was to do the will of God, yet Moses revealed to Israel that after he was gone and they could not hear his voice any more, they would do foolish things, turning away from God. But God would be faithful, allowing terrible things to happen to them so that they would then think about Him and He could help them.

Moses reveals that God wishes the Israelites would do right.

> O that they were wise, that they understood this, that they would consider their latter end! How should one chase a thousand, and two put ten thousand to flight, except their Rock had sold them, and the Lord had shut them up? (Deut. 32:29–30).

If they had walked in the way of God it would have been easy for them to be blessed, but now they needed to learn the hard way. In judgment God would bring calamity to arouse them to see the futility of what they were doing and the foolishness of their ways. God would actually bring all this trouble upon them for the sake of turning them to Him.

In the latter part of this chapter Moses is warned to get ready to die, and thus we are brought face to face with one of the facts of life: even the greatest servant must die.

THE END OF MOSES' MINISTRY
(Deuteronomy 32:44–52)

Do you realize all things come to an end in this world?

Time is limited for everything in this world; only eternity is forever. It is easy for us to feel that now is for always, and sometimes, when we are in the midst of pleasure, it is easy to think it will never end. Sometimes when we are with friends it is just as though we did not ever expect anything to happen except joy and pleasure, but that is not true. On the other hand, there are times when we have sorrow and grief and perhaps pain, and it seems to us the hours last forever. But things do come to an end. We remember the passage, "For the things concerning me have an end" (Luke 22:37). How wise it is for us to remember this and pray the prayer of the psalmist, "So teach us to number our days, that we may apply our hearts unto wisdom" (Ps. 90:12).

Perhaps nowhere is it more important for us to realize that our time is limited than in spiritual matters. We should heed the word that now is the time; today is the day of salvation. We cannot change yesterday, it is in the record; and we cannot build on tomorrow because we haven't reached it yet. The only time we have is now, and if we ever turn to God it should be now.

Some years ago a Mexican doctor said something to me that I have not forgotten. He had asked if a certain sermon I had preached was on record and I told him we had it on tape recording. He then said it would be wonderful to have it in Spanish so that it could be shared. When I said that some day we would have it in Spanish he said, "Some day? Today is the day of salvation; now is the time."

In Deuteronomy 32:44–47 Moses emphasizes the very truth we have been discussing.

> And Moses came and spake all the words of this song in the ears of the people. . . And Moses made an end of speaking all these words to all Israel (Deut. 32:44–45).

He had been with Israel for forty years, and they had heard him many times. He had often instructed and guided them, but this was the last time. He seemed to realize the importance of this as his final message. These are his last words to them:

> And he said unto them, Set your hearts unto all the words which I testify among you this day, which ye shall command your children to observe to do, all the words of this law (Deut. 32:46).

Let us take the Bible and hold its words close to our hearts, committing ourselves to them. As we have opportunity, let us teach them to other people, especially to our own families.

> For it is not a vain thing for you; because it is your life: and through this thing ye shall prolong your days in the land, whither ye go over Jordan to possess it (Deut. 32:47).

Taking up the things of the Lord is a matter of life and death: we come to God or we do not come to God; we walk with God or we do not walk with God. No decision is more important. Moses was involved in arranging his own funeral.

> And the Lord spake unto Moses that selfsame day, saying, Get thee up into this mountain Abarim, unto mount Nebo . . . and die in the mount whither thou goest up, and be gathered unto thy people; as Aaron thy brother died in mount Hor, and was gathered unto his people: because ye trespassed against me among the children of Israel at the waters of Meribah-Kadesh, in the wilderness of Zin; because ye sanctified me not in the midst of the children of Israel. Yet thou shalt see the land before thee; but thou shalt not go thither unto the land which I give the children of Israel (Deut. 32:48–52).

Moses was prepared to leave this world. There may have been nothing glorious about the way he died, but I am satisfied that

Moses was glad to have it that way. Moses spent his lifetime serving the Lord, and he served well. As his day was coming to a close and he prepared to enter the very presence of God, the last words he spoke to the people were, "Set your hearts unto all the words which I testify among you this day" (Deut. 32:46). He told Israel to take these words into their hearts and tell them to their children. Nothing was more important than their decision to obey God. Yes, the things in this world come to an end, but the things of God are forever.

CHAPTERS 33 and 34

✝ ✝ ✝

THE BLESSING OF MOSES
(Deuteronomy 33:1–25)

Does it make any difference if a godly person prays for you?

The people of God have often been blessed by the presence among them of faithful servants of God, just as many congregations are blessed because of faithful ministers. Perhaps you have been in a church like that or perhaps in your own family there is some spiritual person your heart and mind depends upon. What a blessing that can be! We remember how, in Old Testament times, Abraham prayed for Lot, his nephew. After they had been together for some time, they separated on account of quarreling among their servants. Lot went one way, choosing the well-watered plains of Sodom, and Abraham went the other way into the mountains of the plain of Mamre where he built an altar unto God. Later when Lot got into trouble in Sodom, God told Abraham. Abraham prayed for Lot and also for Sodom, trying to convince God to spare the whole city. Later we read this remarkable record: ". . . God remembered Abraham, and sent Lot out of the midst of the overthrow" (Gen. 19:29). God delivered Lot, and that is a challenge to any friend, parent, or pastor.

This ministry of prayer may account for the continuing presence of some godly soul who would be glad to leave this world. I have in mind an elderly friend who is a semi-invalid; all of the members of his family are now gone, and he wants to go to be with the Lord. He prays each night for everyone he knows. I tell him he is being left in the world that others might be blessed, as he continues to pray. Something of this truth is to be seen as Moses came to the end of his ministry.

Moses blessed the people of Israel when he came to the end

of his days. Deuteronomy 33 begins with praise to God. Prayer in the Bible often begins with praise or thanksgiving to God.

> And this is the blessing, wherewith Moses the man of God blessed the children of Israel before his death. And he said, The Lord came from Sinai, and rose up from Seir unto them; he shined forth from mount Paran, and he came with ten thousands of saints: from his right hand went a fiery law for them. Yea, he loved the people; all his saints are in thy hand: and they sat down at thy feet; every one shall receive of thy words (Deut. 33:1–3).

Then follows one statement after another of blessing upon the people. For example, about Reuben it is said, "Let Reuben live, and not die; and let not his men be few" (Deut. 33:6). These blessings are prayers for individual groups of persons. We find that each prayer is different, but I do not think they are necessarily exclusive. I believe Moses would have been glad to have all the tribes blessed in every way, but he did mention specific ones, and this may have some significance.

> . . . let his hands be sufficient for him; and be thou a help to him from his enemies (Deut. 33:7).

In praying for Levi, Moses recognizes Levi's faithfulness in serving the Lord. Something is written about Levi that reminds us of what is written in the New Testament.

> Who said unto his father and to his mother, I have not seen him; neither did he acknowledge his brethren, nor knew his own children (Deut. 33:9).

On one occasion, when people came to Jesus and told Him that His mother and brethren were standing outside, wanting to speak to Him, He answered, "Who is my mother? and who are my brethren?" (Matt. 12:48). It seems here that in Levi's zeal for his ministry, in his faithfulness in service as a priest in the tabernacle, he let no family ties stand in his way of serving God.

Benjamin is also given special reference. He was favored of the Lord.

> The beloved of the Lord shall dwell in safety by him; and the Lord shall cover him all the day long, and he shall dwell between his shoulders (Deut. 33:12).

The longest of all the blessings concerns Joseph. Moses prayed, "Blessed of the Lord be his land," and he enumerates various descriptions of the riches of the blessing. Joseph did not have a tribe in his own name, but his two sons, Ephraim and Manasseh, each had a tribe. Ephraim's tribe was much bigger than Manasseh's. "They are the ten thousands of Ephraim, and they are the thousands of Manasseh" (Deut. 33:17). This is the blessing that came upon Joseph.

> And of Zebulun he said, Rejoice, Zebulun, in thy going out; and, Issachar, in thy tents (Deut. 33:18).

Zebulun is to rejoice in going out, and Issachar is to rejoice in staying at home. As I remarked before this need not mean the blessings are exclusive; all the tribes could rejoice in this way.

About Gad it is written, "Blessed be he that enlargeth Gad" (Deut. 33:20), and "Dan is a lion's whelp: he shall leap from Bashan" (Deut. 33:22). Moses also prayed that "Naphtali [be] satisfied with favour" (Deut. 33:23) and "Asher be blessed with children" (Deut. 33:24). Then comes the wonderful word in connection with Asher, "As thy days, so shall thy strength be" (Deut. 33:25). Blessing was to come upon each of these people. Each was a little different from the other, but each was favored of God. This is the way God treats you and me.

Simeon is omitted from the list. When we look back in Genesis 49 we read that Simeon was involved in an act of cruelty. Because of that there was a very stern word spoken about him there, and his name is omitted here.

THE ETERNAL GOD IS THY REFUGE
(Deuteronomy 33:26–29)

Would you know why a spiritual person can have peace at any time?

The most vital aspect of salvation is the inner relationship with God, the sense of being reconciled to Him and having fellowship with Him. Also important is that God takes a hand in all the affairs that involve His people. Although God works out His plan here on earth, His strength comes out of the spiritual world, out of heaven. He brings the resources of the spiritual world to be our help here and now.

In the closing verses of this chapter of Deuteronomy, Moses reveals to Israel one of the most wonderful promises of assurance in the Bible: "The eternal God is thy refuge, and underneath are the everlasting arms" (Deut. 33:27). God is like a shelter in the time of a storm where I would be safe from danger. If a strange dog comes into the yard where a young child is playing, the child runs into the house and shuts the door; this is his refuge. The believer does not even have to run for safety because "underneath are the everlasting arms." When the believer is too burdened to stand because of the pressure that is upon him, God's everlasting arms are underneath to hold him up.

> Israel then shall dwell in safety alone: the fountain of Jacob shall be upon a land of corn and wine; also his heavens shall drop down dew. Happy art thou, O Israel: who is like unto thee, O people saved by the Lord, the shield of thy help, and who is the sword of thy excellency! and thine enemies shall be found liars unto thee; and thou shalt tread upon their high places" (Deut. 33:28–29).

This passage pictures a people who have been in danger of enemies trying to destroy them. Having passed through a time of peril and of threat, they have turned to the Lord and suddenly found that He will take care of them. The testimony they give to the world is ". . . O people *saved* by the Lord." We should understand the word *saved* and ask ourselves: "Am I a saved person?" There are many definitions of the word *saved*, but our meaning is found in Scripture. We should let the Bible tell us about the word because it refers to what God will do for us in Christ Jesus. I know He will save me from destruction and that He will save me from punishment because of my sins. More than that, He will save me from my weakness and into fellowship with Himself. The word *saved* refers to everything that Christ Jesus does for us. I have found help in understanding the word by putting an *l* in it to make it *salved*, (which means healed and comforted).

Moses reminds Israel that the Lord is the shield of their help, and the word of their excellency!" The shield of help is for protection, and the sword of excellency is a weapon for attack, an instrument of efficiency. Perhaps there are those who feel they do not have enemies. But I'm not referring only to human enemies; Satan is the enemy of all men's souls. We are beset on every side by things that try to shake our confidence, and things happen all the time to make us fret. These are enemies that we can have victory over in the Lord Jesus Christ.

Because the eternal God is our refuge and underneath are His everlasting arms we can be saved and victorious all the time.

THE DEATH OF MOSES
(Deuteronomy 34)

Are you conscious of the fact that you are responsible for sharing salvation with others?

God is a rewarder of them that diligently seek Him. A person will either turn to God or will not turn to God. If he does turn to God, God will receive him; if he does not turn to God he will be distressed and shut out from Him. There is no use for the man to say, "I don't want it that way" because that is the way it is; he has one life and that one life can be saved or lost. And there is only one Savior, Jesus Christ. "There is none other name under heaven given among men, whereby we must be saved" (Acts 4:12).

There is one gospel that we can share with others, and that gospel is being preached today throughout the world in over a thousand languages. Everywhere people are being told:

> For God so loved the world, that he gave his only begotten Son, that whosoever believeth in him should not perish, but have everlasting life (John 3:16).

In our study we have been noticing especially God's instruction for blessing. God's man, Moses, was the servant who led the children of Israel, and in Moses' heart were all God's blessings for Israel.

> And Joshua the son of Nun was full of the spirit of wisdom; for
> Moses had laid his hands upon him: and the children of Israel
> hearkened unto him, and did as the Lord commanded Moses
> (Deut. 34:9).

The laying on of the hands of Moses implied that Moses had shared with Joshua his own spirit and had given to Joshua his personal blessing. Joshua would now lead Israel. There is no evidence that there was any personal selfishness on Moses' part. He was glad to relinquish the leadership into Joshua's hands and to share his own grace and mercy with him so that Joshua could continue to bless the people.

> And there arose not a prophet since in Israel like unto Moses,
> whom the Lord knew face to face (Deut. 34:10).

We would say that Moses was great because he knew and obeyed God, and because he knew God he received guidance and encouragement. But did you notice that is not what the Scripture says? It says "the Lord knew him." *Knew* means more than just acquainted with. It has in it the idea of accepting, respecting, and sharing with.

Scripture says, "There arose not a prophet since in Israel like unto Moses." There was no other to bring the people out of Egypt, dealing with opposing forces with a mighty hand, and leading Israel through the wilderness and on into the land of Canaan. God knew and used Moses. Something else is said about Moses we should not miss: he was 120 years old when he died and "His eye was not dim, nor his natural force abated" (Deut. 34:7).

He must have been a great and strong man humanly speaking, but we know that his strength came from God. Moses was a servant of God, and in Deuteronomy we are told nothing about his personal human abilities. All we see is a faithful man of God who served Him that the people might come to know God and to do His will.

NOT A PROPHET SINCE LIKE MOSES
(Deuteronomy 34)

Have you ever realized how much you depend on some people?

No man lives to himself; we are all involved with other people. Were it not for other people we could not live. How pathetic it is when a person fails to realize this enough to keep him humble. Everything we use to sustain life, or for our welfare or happiness, has been provided for us. Some people are particularly special. For example, what would your life be if it had not been for your parents? Maybe there is a pastor from whom you have received a great deal of help, or perhaps you have a friend who prays and cares for you.

Moses took an active part in training and preparing Israel for entering the Promised Land. When he first began trying to help the people, when he was sent by God to bring them out of Egypt, Moses had the greatest responsibility of all servants of the Lord. This comes to mind when we note what the Scriptures say about Moses' death.

> And Moses went up from the plains of Moab unto the mountain of Nebo. . . . And the Lord said unto him, This is the land which I sware unto Abraham, unto Isaac, and unto Jacob, saying I will give it unto thy seed: I have caused thee to see it with thine eyes, but thou shalt not go over thither (Deut. 34:1–4).

God had previously told Moses that he would not enter Canaan, so this must have weighed heavy on Moses' heart.

> So Moses the servant of the Lord died there in the land of Moab, according to the word of the Lord (Deut. 34:5).

The title "Moses the servant of the Lord" must have been precious to Moses. He was the leader of the people, but he never counted himself to be the servant of the people. He led them, was meek and humble before them, and he suffered many things because of them, but he never was the servant of the people. Rather he was the servant of the Lord. He wasn't even his own. He had no schemes to get rich and no plan to get ahead; he did not even think of building himself up. His whole interest was in being a servant of the Lord.

So Moses, the servant of the Lord, died there in the land of Moab according to the word of the Lord.

> And he buried him in a valley in the land of Moab, over against Bethpeor: but no man knoweth of his sepulcher unto this day (Deut. 34:6).

This is an important passage of Scripture because it tells us that no one knows where Moses was buried. There was one man since the flood who was not buried anywhere, and that was Elijah. Elijah was taken up into the presence of God and so was never buried anywhere here on earth. Moses passed away in the mountain of Nebo, and we are told that the Lord took care of him. We may get the impression that the Lord had buried Moses, as here we read that "He buried him in a valley in the land of Moab, but no man knoweth of his sepulcher unto this day."

Some students of the Bible wonder whether that burial had to do with leaving his body in this world at all. The reason for questioning earthly burial is that when our Lord Jesus Christ was transfigured there were two men with Him—Moses and Elijah. We know that Elijah's body never saw corruption in this world, because it was taken out of this world. And some people wonder about Moses. There is one other rare obscure passage in the New Testament which says that when Michael the archangel strove with Satan over the body of Moses he could only say, "The Lord rebuke thee" (Jude 1:9). It appears that there was something strange about the disposal of his body. But I am sure this is not the most important point. What is important is that Moses was the Lord's servant; he lived his life as unto God, and when he died, he died as unto God. And God took care of him. Amen.